Moroney's detailed and rich self-analysis of his own contact experience is unique among such literature. His analysis of the UFO abduction scenario raises many questions, and he makes observations and comments that challenge traditional views within not only ufology, but our society and view of ourselves in the universe. Whether or not we believe such experiences are real, the contactee phenomenon, as laid out in Moroney's work, deserves consideration. The spiritual component of the contactee experience is something that must be addressed, and Moroney's reasoning why this is so supports this viewpoint.

Chris Rutkowski
science writer and
author of *A World of UFOs*

THE EXTRATERRESTRIAL
ANSWER
BOOK

UFOs, Alien Adbuctions,
and the Coming ET Presence

JIM MORONEY

HAMPTON ROADS
PUBLISHING COMPANY, INC.

Cover design by Steve Amarillo
Cover art by © Jeff Vanuga/Corbis
Illustrations by Ralph Hagen
www.hagenstoons.com
www.aufosg.com

Hampton Roads Publishing Company, Inc.
Charlottesville, VA 22906
www.hrpub.com

Library of Congress Cataloging-in-Publication Data

Moroney, Jim, 1960-
The extraterrestrial answer book : UFOs, alien abductions, and the
coming ET presence / Jim Moroney.
    p. cm.
Summary: "We are not alone. Covering topics from the scientific
evidence that aliens exist to what the government should do about
them to why they are here in the first place, this book provides specific
instructions on how to handle an extraterrestrial encounter"—Provided by publisher.
    Includes bibliographical references and index.
    ISBN 978-1-57174-620-7 (5.25 x 7.25 tp : alk. paper)
    1. Human-alien encounters. I. Title.
    BF2050.M663 2009
    001.942--dc22
                                        2009032967

ISBN 978-1-57174-620-7
10 9 8 7 6 5 4 3 2 1
Printed on acid-free paper in the United States

To all those I love (you know who you are).

TABLE OF CONTENTS

FOREWORD

"Sometimes I think we're alone in the universe, and sometimes I think we're not. In either case the idea is quite staggering."
—Arthur C. Clarke, author of 2001: A Space Odyssey

Just about the only thing I can say with certainty about the aliens is that they come from a very different world from ours. It's a world so fundamentally different that I'm not sure we'll ever fully understand them or their purposes. Sobering as that thought may be, I'm still convinced that we must at least try to understand them and meet them halfway. Our future and the future of this planet likely depend on it.

So far, our collective response to their existence has been abysmal at best. This must change.

There are two main types of interaction between the aliens and humans. The first type of interaction involves visual sightings of unidentified flying objects (UFOs) or the physical traces they leave behind. The second type of interaction involves direct contact, sometimes including the abduction of one or more human beings. While the aliens may have a rather casual attitude regarding who sees their craft, their attitude towards human contact is anything but casual. Not only do they appear to be very deliberate about their choice of contactees, they're quite careful to control what each contactee remembers, and the timing under which these memories are allowed to surface.

For whatever reason, I'm one of the millions of people world wide who have been contacted. This contact has presented some of the greatest emotional, intellectual, and spiritual challenges of my life. In spite of that, I do not feel as if I've been a victim. Since 1987, I've immersed myself in the study, understanding, and, ultimately, the acceptance of this great mystery. This book is the result of my personal struggle and journey into a greater reality that all of us will have to face eventually.

Even after twenty years, it *is* still a struggle and the journey is nowhere near its end. To ponder the question of whether or not other living beings exist is one thing; to *know* that they exist and that they can choose to show up in your home at any time for some purpose that you don't fully understand is something altogether different.

The ramifications can be intensely personal. Do you ever again have a truly private moment? Are you at risk during the contact experiences? Can the process harm you? Will you be able to effectively cope with the experiences? If you're dating someone, what do you tell them, and when? If you marry, are you placing your partner at risk? What in heaven's name do you tell your children? What does it *mean* that you're exposing your family to this phenomenon? Will they be abducted too, in which case disclosure and sharing might make life easier for everyone—or might just scare the heck out of them for no good reason (or at worst, risk having your beloved children convinced that you're a "bit of a nut case")? What does it mean for your professional career, for your friendships?

In 1991, the Roper Organization, a US polling organization, asked 5,947 American adults a series of questions that might indicate an abduction experience. The results (described in detail in chapter 3), which were considered to represent the experiences of 185,000,000 US adults, showed that 2 percent of study participants could well be experiencing contact. Two percent of 185,000,000 people is about 3,700,000 Americans; this estimate doesn't even include the rest of the world! It's only fair to point out that any attempt to estimate the number of people having contact is fraught with logistical and scientific uncertainties. We still lack a definitive way of quantifying who has and has not had contact. Despite the uncertainty and controversy surrounding the subject, we can be relatively certain of one thing: the number of people having contact experiences is going to increase.

When it comes to studying the aliens, there's a lot of conflicting information—not to mention misinformation, disinformation, and pure bunk—to wade through. Because of my role in the Alberta UFO study group (a local organization that gathers sighting data), I'm fairly accessible to the general public. Occasionally someone will call to report that they or someone they know has had an abduction experience. Most of them are normal people reporting legitimate experiences; people who just want someone to talk to about the extraordinary events they've been part of.

However, there are times that I'm convinced, after listening, that the person did *not*, in fact, have a contact experience. In such cases, I believe it's in the person's best interests for me to be honest, even though they may not like what I have to say. It's much easier to discern what's real and what's not in the abduction field once you've been exposed directly to the alien beings. Always, a healthy dose of skepticism is required. This is not to say that everyone's experiences will be the same. Certainly, differences must be expected, but within the wide variety of legitimate experiences, commonalities do emerge.

Over the years, I've come to understand that at the core of

the phenomenon is the aliens' struggle to build a relationship with us. It's a new type of relationship, with a depth and purpose that few have ever experienced within the sphere of human relationships. But if I am right in my conclusions, it's a kind of relationship that many more of us will be experiencing in the future.

Humanity is fast approaching a crisis point. Our surging technological accomplishments have simply outpaced our lagging spiritual development and we have unwittingly become an imminent danger to ourselves and our world. We have invented and accumulated weapons so lethal that we may not survive their deployment. A crisis is coming, and the survival of humanity and most of life on Earth is hanging in the balance. The aliens are here to help us through this crisis. It won't be easy. The relationship feels forced because it's occurring far sooner than it should have. Ideally the contact should have progressed slowly over time, but our collective actions have taken humanity to the brink of global disaster and have made a rapid intervention necessary. The number of changes we'll need in order to achieve a peaceful, environmentally balanced world will be staggering, but I believe that many of us are open to new ideas and ready to take up the challenge. Learning from the aliens will be a critical part of that solution.

The real challenge in writing this book has been to write for the future, not the present. Other authors, most notably Whitley Strieber and the late Harvard professor Dr. John E. Mack, have extensively documented the nature of these contact experiences. The goal of this book is to explore how we as a society—or perhaps as a species—will respond to the challenge that is being placed before us. Although the book includes some of my experiences, it's not about me. It's about all of us and our future.

In writing this book, I've made some assumptions. After studying the experiences of many people and looking for common threads, I've consolidated this understanding into a best guess scenario about the way that the UFO phenomenon is going to evolve, and how we ought to be responding. If we assume that the phenomenon is not going to change in any substantial way from the current pattern, there would be little point in planning a response. However, I believe that we're approaching a major turning point, and we need to be putting certain mechanisms in place to deal with this change.

People ask whether the encounters have changed me. Yes, of course—but in sometimes unexpected ways. I've become more deeply aware of the need to take responsibility for myself as a person. I've learned to take care of myself and try to be the best person I can be. (Not that I'm bucking for a nomination to saint or hero; I'm much too fallible for that. There's a fine line between courage and stupidity, and the truth is, I've ambled down both sides of that line.) I'll admit that I've been scared. After all, I'm just an ordinary person trying to make sense of some extraordinary experiences.

The process has been a roller-coaster ride through almost every conceivable emotion—from terror to fascination to curiosity to incomprehension to embarrassment to overwhelming feelings of connection and love. I've made some dumb mistakes, some of which you'll read about in this book. There have been moments of humor too, things that, in retrospect, are too surreal to be anything but funny. This is one element that is poorly represented in other accounts of contact: these beings definitely have a sense of humor. The humorous passages in this book don't mean that I take what happened lightly. They just happen to be true.

Over the years, I've taught health and safety and occupational hygiene (my profession) courses at a number of colleges and universities. Sometimes as a change of pace during the lectures I'll talk about the UFO phenomenon and ask students what they think. The response to this digression is always overwhelmingly positive. People want to know.

Occasionally I'm criticized for my "beliefs." But there is a crucial difference between what one believes and what one *knows*. I *know* that these beings, and my experiences with them, are real—just as real as the food I eat, the air I breathe, or the car I drive. Direct perceptual experience is dramatically different from a belief. Direct experience creates knowledge, and with knowledge comes the clarity of understanding that brings peace. I don't need to tell everyone about my experiences for the purpose of convincing them of their reality. I'm very sympathetic to the difficulties that some people have in believing in aliens, and I certainly won't condemn those who don't believe they exist. I don't feel a strong need to argue with anyone over what I've experienced.

It sometimes feels like I'm standing on a warm sunny beach, ankle deep in cool water, peering out onto the ocean horizon. I can clearly see a huge wave in the distance rapidly approaching, building and moving with great speed and intensity. Occasionally there is a person facing me, but they can't or won't turn to see the wave. I don't know exactly what will happen when it hits and I'm genuinely concerned about everyone who is standing on the beach with me. All I can do is raise the alarm to those who will listen.

Like a force of nature, the extraterrestrial phenomenon is going to prove itself as the number of sightings continues to increase significantly over the coming years. By the year 2010 or 2020, a much greater proportion of the human race (if not all of us) will be aware, in varying degrees, of the presence of the aliens. The fundamental question will no longer be "Do they exist?" The fundamental questions will be "Who are they?" "How are they interacting with us?" and "How should we respond?"

And yet, very few have tried to explore what will happen after our society openly concludes that there is an extraterrestrial presence on Earth. It's a question that we need to consider, and soon. The global warming issue provides a useful parallel. We knew that global warming was occurring, but its causes, scope, and urgency were unclear until a 2007 UN report on the issue provided the "tipping point" that galvanized public opinion and triggered political action. (Whether or not you believe that the conclusions of the UN report are valid, there is no denying that it triggered political action.) I believe that our relationship with the aliens will undergo a similar defining moment, after which societies and governments will need to act. It's vital that these actions be taken from an informed perspective. For this reason, and acting within a spirit of social responsibility, I have written this book.

I've tried not to rehash old ground that others have covered in depth, unless the information is a necessary context for new ideas. Instead, my goal has been to concentrate on these simple questions: How do we decide what to do about this phenomenon, and how do we do it? The "response planning" component of the book draws heavily on my experiences in municipal government. I've also tried to indicate how the emerging phenomenon is likely to affect individuals, and what they can do to prepare.

The complexity of our relationship with the aliens is enormous. If we're to have any hope of understanding them and learning from them, we must keep open minds about who and what they are. If we're to avoid destroying ourselves, we may well need to redefine who and what *we* are. If there is to be a new world, it will be our generation that will have the greatest difficulty living in it.

To me, one measure of the fullness of a human life is whether that person has had the courage to do what they were created to do, to do the things they know are right, even if it scares the hell out of them. Like writing this book.

But like most other living souls on this planet, I can hope for nothing more than the courage to get up and do my best, to do what I have to do, and let the chips fall where they may. I hope you enjoy the book.

Jim Moroney
January 2009

THROUGH THE LOOKING GLASS

"It is no longer a question of when will humanity interact with extraterrestrials, but rather the much more difficult question of how they have decided to interact with us!"
—Jim Moroney

Before the summer of 1987, I thought I understood the UFO phenomenon. As far back as high school, I'd pondered, in a relaxed sort of way, whether or not extraterrestrial life might exist. Being a science buff, I was deeply interested in the technology surrounding the space program, but as far as the possibility of extraterrestrial life went, I didn't have a strong interest either way. Like many others, I believed that life probably existed beyond this planet. When I first read about UFOs in the 1960s, it didn't seem unreasonable to accept that they were probably out there some-place, even though I'd never seen one. I did (and still do) believe that some UFO reports were fabricated, but it still seemed that there was a core of truth to the whole phenomenon. I assumed that the beings who operated such craft would turn out to be pretty much like humans, just more advanced technologically.

I didn't think much about the aliens' intentions. It even seemed plausible that they had chosen not to interfere directly with our society, but to keep their distance and avoid direct contact. I also thought it would be nice if we were given an opportunity to meet them. However, I didn't think much about how that interaction might occur, whether they'd come down one day and say "take me to your leader," or whether it would be we who went looking for them. Over the years, I had heard reports of abductions. The whole idea seemed unlikely, but I couldn't rule out the possibility that a few unlucky souls might have been captured and cruelly studied by cold, emotionally detached alien beings. In short, there wasn't much information available on the subject, and I operated under the subconscious frame of reference most of us have picked up by watching science fiction programs on TV.

As it turns out, I was completely wrong on almost every point.

My First Conscious Encounter

August 9, 1987, was a cool summer evening. I had taken a few days off to drive from Edmonton, Alberta, to Sarnia, Ontario, to attend my sister's wedding. I'd left Edmonton early the previous afternoon and had driven to Winnipeg, Manitoba, about an eleven- to twelve-hour stretch and over eight hundred miles. As I neared Winnipeg, I began to have a strong premonition that the aliens were around and that our first physical contact might actually occur.

To explain why I felt that way, it's necessary to step back to an event that had occurred a few weeks earlier. As a result of an auto injury, I had taken up meditation to help with soft tissue rehabilitation. A few weeks before the Winnipeg trip, during one of the meditation sessions, an image had suddenly formed in my mind. It began as a close, formless mass, then rapidly drew back to coalesce into a pair of eyes; then, around the eyes, a face. It was a human face. The image grew in clarity to reveal piercing blue eyes and long blonde wavy hair; simply a human female, nothing too remarkable about it. But somehow it was more than just an image. There was a strange sense of presence to it. So I mentally asked, "Who are you?" expecting, perhaps, some insights from my own subconscious.

When she told me her name, I knew that the response was not coming from inside me. I couldn't have pronounced the name, and today I can't entirely remember it, but I have a sense that it was a long name with a high, shrill sound at the end. Almost instantaneously, the face changed, assuming a definitely not-human appearance.

If the name had bewildered me, the change in appearance was positively horrifying. Instinctively, my mind bolted for normal consciousness, but sometimes when you're in a deep meditative state, it can be difficult to snap out of it. While my mind was still pulling away, she surrounded me with an overwhelming feeling of unconditional love and contained within that love was a message that said, "We're here to help you."

The message wasn't verbalized; it was more of a direct connection to my consciousness, during which an idea-image was delivered. The image itself is hard to put into words. In every language, there are words that are so culturally specific that they have no equivalent in other languages. This was an *idea* that had no equivalent within the English language or current human understanding. Within that one idea was simultaneously contained, "Jim, we're here to help you personally, and we're here to help your friends, and we're here to help all of humanity." Her distinction between me and the people around me, both friends and strangers, was much smaller than humans typically make. Rather than viewing each of these three concepts separately, she fused them all into a simultaneous whole, in which the individual components were not blurred or lost, but united. The message itself was clear: "This is what we're doing."

Understandably, when my mind did struggle free of the meditative state, I was stunned, shocked, and elated, literally holding my head and jumping around the room yelling, "Oh my God! Did I just blow a circuit?" I could still feel that overwhelming, unconditional love. I regretted that I hadn't stayed with her (whatever she was) longer, but the sudden shock of her transformation to an alien appearance had propelled me into full waking consciousness. I might have dismissed the whole thing as an artifact of meditation, if it hadn't been for that overpowering, exhilarating, lingering sense of love. It made the whole experience far too real to ignore.

Over the next two weeks, I kept thinking about the experience. Should I tell anyone? Of course not; who would believe me? Still, I couldn't help feeling that *something*, some further contact, was going to happen. I just *knew* it.

I started to recall earlier experiences when I'd awakened with a feeling of paralysis and a perception that something (someone?) had been in the room. Were these experiences related? What would happen next? The sense of unconditional love and overwhelming peace still lingered, wrapping itself around me like a warm comfortable blanket. It was so *real*. I wanted more. I wanted to initiate a meaningful dialogue with this being, whoever or whatever she was.

How could I have predicted that the next encounter was going to utterly devastate me and strip away virtually everything I thought I knew about the world I lived in?

A Full-Blown Encounter

As I drove toward Winnipeg that August night, the premonition that something was about to happen kept getting stronger.

It was totally unlike anything I'd ever felt before. Something was going to happen—and something inside me knew it.

I drove through the darkness thinking *why me?* I was no representative of anything important. What did they want with me? What would happen? What would I see? I was thinking clearly enough to realize that if I really was about to contact a more advanced species, the greater risk would come from my actions, not theirs. They probably knew a lot more about humanity than I knew about them. If something happened that scared me, would I be able to control my fear? What if I couldn't? Might I panic and somehow endanger my own life? I was determined to be the best possible representative for "friendly humanity" but the more I contemplated the potential risks and unknowns, the more the whole thing started to feel like an impending disaster.

I thought about pulling off onto an old, dusty, dirt side road and trying to sleep, but one glance down the dark, empty road convinced me to look for a less isolated location. Driving deeper into the night, I decided that however events played out, the first seconds would be critical. I had to try to demonstrate that I meant them no harm. Easier said than done; I was seriously worried about losing control and freaking out, which might place me in grave danger. I decided that maybe the best thing to do would be to keep my eyes closed for part of the experience. By reducing and controlling the amount of sensory input, I might be able to reduce the fear so I could manage the situation more calmly.

By that time, the uneasiness had deepened into something approaching dread. *But was this even real?* This is crazy. The being was so loving . . . why am I getting so uneasy? Maybe it was all in my head. I did know, however, that thoughts of stopping anywhere in the dark had long since passed. Nearing exhaustion, I pulled into a truck stop called Deacon's Corner outside of Winnipeg off Highway 1. There were a couple of rigs parked to the side of the friendly little diner. I pulled into an empty space in front, slid over to the passenger side to get the steering wheel and foot pedals out of the way, put the seat back, closed my eyes, and tried to get comfortable. I had originally intended to leave the windows open, but the coolness of the night combined with the incessant local mosquitoes soon enticed me to completely roll up the windows.

Although I hadn't known it when I pulled in, truck stops are not necessarily the best places to try to sleep. Sleeping in a big rig in a warm bed with curtains is one thing. Sleeping in a little Honda Civic near these goliaths is something else altogether. Mammoth rigs would shake my makeshift bedroom and illuminate it like I was staring into a midday sun.

So there I was, lying on my back with my eyes closed, and along came *another* transport truck. *He must be pulling in,* I thought, because those huge, bright headlights were blasting right into my car again. Then I realized that one of the lights was blue—and *the lights were moving over the top of the car and were now exploding through my sunroof.*

Oh God, here we go, I thought, eyes tightly shut, wondering if anyone in the diner was seeing this.

The air went dead, as if its density had suddenly changed. I could hear the rpms of a nearby truck engine dropping slightly, but the sound was becoming increasingly faint. It was as if something were inhibiting the transmission of sound energy through the surrounding air. The next two things happened simultaneously: a sudden paralysis and an absolute, overwhelming sense of terror. Instantly, I recognized the paralysis as the same kind of paralysis that I had experienced at various points in my lifetime, but this time it was more intense and longer-lasting. It was shocking to realize that those earlier episodes of paralysis had actually been caused by the aliens, and that they must have been in contact with me for years, without my ever knowing it! The fear was sudden, stark, overwhelming, and totally unexpected. It just came out of nowhere, a terror so crushing that it made it difficult to analyze the situation or respond in a controlled way. (After additional contact experiences, I have concluded that the fear is probably biologically induced by the paralysis, as some sort of side effect.)

The hair on my arms began to rise, but I still didn't open my eyes. It seemed as if I was in some kind of strong electromagnetic field, perhaps created by the propulsion system of the silent, brilliantly lit craft that I knew must be hovering above the car. Then something brushed against my right arm. Even though my eyes were still closed, my other senses said that I was still in the car. But I had closed all the windows! That meant that the object now touching my arm could only have entered by passing *straight through solid material.*

The gentle movement against my arm had stopped, almost as if they were waiting for me to do something. It certainly occurred to me that my life might well depend on what I did next. I still hadn't opened my eyes. At this point, I didn't think I could handle seeing some kind of creature peering at me. I didn't want to lose the small amount of self-control that I was clinging to and do something stupid that might jeopardize my life.

While this was happening, I was struggling against a terror so intense that it threatened to overwhelm my rational, conscious mind. Nonetheless, I somehow managed to form the thought that I had to do *something* to show that I meant them no harm and was willing to communicate. But I literally could not speak. I couldn't move, not even my mouth! They were using such an extraordinary amount of force to restrain me that I quickly reasoned they must be afraid of me. This wasn't good! The situation was deteriorating rapidly. Maybe I could unlock the door and open it, I thought. Maybe that would convey to them that I wanted to communicate with them and was no threat. With immense mental and physical effort, I managed to slowly move my right arm through that endless few inches and unlock the door. It was so exhausting that the moment I succeeded, my arm dropped like a thousand-pound lead weight.

Then I began to feel a pressing sensation around my head, as if some kind of band were being tightened—not an actual, physical band, but some kind of energy force that was putting pressure on my head. As the pressure increased, I felt my consciousness drift further and further back into a state of deep relaxation. The fear was dissipating, but any kind of resistance to the pressure caused an immediate and painful throbbing.

At this point, the memories become jumbled and disconnected . . . I was in a different position and could hear an echo of myself screaming . . . I was lying down and could feel something touch me behind the right ear, sending what felt like an electrical shock into my brain. It felt as if the object that touched me was both mechanical and alive. I could feel waves of energy dissipating into my brain, branching out along specific pathways . . . suddenly I was back in the car, and as the paralysis began to vanish, the lights began to move off to the right.

Two months would pass before I would have the courage to attempt to uncover what had actually happened during this episode and the piece of time of which I had no memory.

Now What?

One of the dangers of being a contactee is that if you're not careful, your encounter-world can start to seem more important than life here on Earth. Some contactees report an overwhelming sense of mission, thinking that they've been chosen for contact because there is something humanity is supposed to be *doing*. However, such responses usually come later in the overall process. Initially, most contactees have their hands full just trying to assimilate their new experiences.

I was no exception. It's fair to say that my own contact experiences have destroyed not only every preconceived idea I've ever had about aliens, but also my fundamental beliefs about reality and humanity's place in the universe. I've been given glimpses of a greater reality so overwhelming that it has literally shattered the carefully assembled belief system that our society calls "reality." There is no way that anyone could have prepared me for what these contact experiences would do. The beings I've encountered and the realities I've glimpsed have been overwhelming beyond my wildest imagination.

After that first contact in 1987, it seemed that any effort to convince other people of what had happened would be futile. I had no physical evidence that would stand up to any scientific inquiry, and no basis for explaining the psychological components of the experience.

The night of that first physical encounter, I simply kept moving. I drove all night and slept during the day. I didn't want to sleep at night. When I reached Ontario, I didn't tell my family what had happened. My sister's wedding went off without a hitch, but days afterward, I was still agitated and tense.

I had to talk to someone. Finally I sat down with my sister and said, "Look, I don't know how you're going to take this, but . . . ," and I couldn't continue. I simply could not speak. Instead, I started to cry. Our family is very loving, but we normally don't show strong emotions unless there's a serious matter involved, so, understandably, my sister was upset by my behavior. What surprised me was how deeply upset I was. I'd managed to function at a reasonable level over the previous few days, but now the repressed feelings just came rushing out. I managed to blurt out that I had had an abduction experience or an encounter experience. I said that I knew it sounded insane, but it had happened.

My sister said something very profound. She said, "Okay, Jim. How does this affect me?" Although this may sound callous, I'm convinced that it wasn't meant that way. She was simply pointing out that I had not considered how my disclosing this information would affect other people. I realized that I hadn't really thought about how the information might affect other people, or whether it would affect them at all. It's as if a voice inside my head suddenly said, "Jim, this is *your* experience and you're going to have to come to terms with it on your own." Talking with my sister helped, but I realized that the work of understanding had to take place inside my own head. I had to find my own answers.

One answer that I needed was the answer to what had happened to me during the missing period of time during the encounter. I remembered the band squeezing my head. I remembered the probe touching me behind the ear. I remembered waking up in the car. What had happened in between? Not knowing that answer was like watching a movie with a major scene missing. Except that the movie was my life and not knowing what was in that missing scene was intolerable.

I considered hypnosis. For a contactee, undergoing hypnosis is like opening up Pandora's box. You have absolutely no idea what's in there, and some of it could be very, very frightening. Why open the box at all? Do you really need bigger issues to deal with than you already have?

To know . . . or not to know? I obsessed over that question for every waking second of every day for the two months it ultimately took me to decide to undergo hypnosis. Part of me had to know; another part of me was terrified beyond reason. Finally, I decided to do it, because it was becoming increasingly clear that I could never live with the agitation and uncertainty if I didn't. Also, it's my nature to be curious. Maybe the ultimate reason was that I simply had to find out.

The answers were staggering.

All Is Revealed

After unlocking the car door to signal the aliens that I was willing to meet them, I felt myself moving forward and upward, out of the car seat. The movement was accompanied by an excruciating pain, as if every fiber in my body were being torn apart. For a moment, it felt as if I were being ripped to pieces. The searing pain was agonizing. If I'd been able to open my mouth to scream, I would have.

Then, just as abruptly as it started, the pain stopped and I was standing beside my car inside a 50-foot diameter, circular, amphitheater-type of room with tiered steps. Each step in the tier was about 5 inches high and 2 feet deep, which would be rather odd step spacing for humans. On the steps stood six stoic identical-looking beings, all dressed in a kind of uniform. They had the typical large heads that many contactees have described and stood about four-and-a-half feet tall. The atmosphere was filled with tension as they all intently stared at me.

I promptly started *yelling* at them.

In retrospect, the stupidity of my response astounds me. The searing pain may have disappeared, but the lingering fear that I had been about to die was still present. They had floated me out through the front of the car, right through the dashboard, and I assumed that this passage through solid material was the cause of the pain. (Later, when they floated me through some other solid objects, I found out that it wasn't. But I didn't know that at the time, and the residual impact of the pain was still very fresh, so even though I was scared, I wanted to take control of the situation to prevent another callous act on their part.)

So I started screaming at them. And *swearing*. (So here's Jim, who was committed to not doing anything that might endanger his life, and who had intended to be a top-notch ambassador for the human race, screaming things like, "You could have used the fucking door! I unlocked the fucking thing for you! I did all this shit so that I can *talk* to you guys, and you fucking hurt me! What do you think you're doing!!!?")

Upon which, one of the beings stepped forward and asked, "What do you need doors for?"

What did we need doors for? My surprise at hearing the response spoken in perfect English was lost in the jaw-dropping strangeness of the moment. What did we need *doors* for? Oh God—how was I going to communicate with these little bastards if the cultural gap was so huge that we didn't even have *doors* in common? I was getting angry again when another one of the beings stepped forward, and suddenly, in the next instant, I was completely calm. It was obvious that they had the ability to exert direct influence on my emotional state.

I asked them if the alien being who had contacted me during my meditation was also on the ship. I can't remember her name now, but at the time I did, saying, "Is Althenia here?"

There was a split second of hesitation, a quick glance at each other, and all six of them burst out laughing. The oppressive tension of the moment was suddenly broken by my inability to pronounce her name. I wonder what they thought was so funny. They were literally in stitches and barely able to contain themselves.

Apparently I had mangled her name quite hopelessly, and that's why they were laughing. Imagine, if you will, one emotionally tattered human being facing six small, decidedly nonhuman beings, all of whom are laughing hysterically. *So much*, I thought, *for intergalactic relations.*

I assumed they were laughing at my stupidity. Without thinking, I said, "Okay, go ahead and laugh at me, I'm just the stupid human." And one of them, still struggling for composure, said, "No, no, it's not you, her name is &^%$*#." (I still can't recall her actual name.) As it turned out, she was on the ship somewhere. When she contacted me through the meditation, she must have already been planning this physical contact. I now suspect that she gave them a stern briefing on how she contacted me, how important it was, what they needed to do, how to do it, what not to do, when to do it, and so on. Obviously, it seemed funny that she didn't manage to provide me with her name in a way I could remember.

Two of the beings told me to come with them. With one walking in front and one behind, I was escorted to what appeared to be a shower facility. Inside the chamber, but fully clothed, I was subjected to a blast of light combined with something else that I couldn't identify. I was relieved that I didn't have to remove my clothes but it was certainly uncomfortable, and I assumed it was some kind of decontamination chamber.

Next, we walked down a hallway. I noticed a certain automatic compliance in my own reactions, as if I were no longer in complete conscious control of myself. They gave me suggestions and I followed them. It seemed perfectly natural to do what I was told. At no time while I was in the craft did I have any sense of it being in motion, although I suspect that it was. It's also notable that all the beings who spoke to me demonstrated a flawless command of the English language although most used very short phrases. I don't recall them speaking any words or initiating any verbal or auditory communication between themselves.

Inside the Ship

As we walked, I did have the presence of mind to make some mental notes about what I was seeing. The hallways were about 7 feet wide, with the walls curved so they were slightly wider in the middle than at the top and bottom. Three people could easily have walked abreast in them. The halls had narrow support archways spaced about every ten feet.

The lighting in the hallway was indirect but bright. The light source was in the floor, but I couldn't see the actual source, just a glow of light similar to a track-lighting system. The ceiling was about 8 feet high, although I soon found out that it was higher in other areas of the structure. We crossed an intersecting hallway. Notably, the intersection was a perfect 90-degree angle. The hallway we crossed was about 35 feet long, with only one door opening off it. That hallway appeared to connect to another hallway running parallel to the one I was walking on. The cumulative suggestion of these details was that there was one large compartment in the intervening space. There were no windows, so I couldn't determine my location in the structure, or the relative size of the vessel. It felt like a very large craft. (I now think that I may have been picked up by a smaller craft and taken to this larger one.)

Many of the design concepts seemed to reflect human architecture. The general air temperature (about 22 degrees Celsius) and air quality were completely consistent with a large, well-ventilated Earth building. However, there was no sense of air movement, no unusual odors, and no visible indication of a heating, ventilation, or air-conditioning system. As far as I could tell, the gravitational field strength was normal. I looked at the small being walking ahead of me. How likely would it be to find an alien species that would prefer the exact same environment that humans thrived in? I compared the diminutive size of all the beings I'd seen with the human-sized dimensions of the ship. The implications were staggering. The ship must have been constructed for the purpose of dealing with human beings. It was very unlikely that I was the first person to be here, I thought. The colossal commitment to resources, design, and function was astonishing. What in the world are they doing with us?

As I walked, I had time to study the head of the being walking ahead of me. It was large, bald, bi-lobed, and I could distinctly see large arteries or veins pulsating beneath the thin skin. I didn't count the pulse rate, but there must have been a huge blood flow to the brain to create that kind of visible pulsing. The neck seemed far too small to effectively support the head, suggesting either a completely different internal structure from humans, or some sort of localized independence from the Earth's gravitational field. In spite of their small necks and relatively large head-to-body size ratio, they moved with utter ease.

Without warning, I had the most disturbing, overwhelming urge to bite into the head in front of me and eat it like an apple. It was a powerful impulse, as if I really needed to taste that head. A metaphor from my subconscious, telling me to fully taste this experience? Who knows; maybe it was just the guy behind me playing a joke on his buddy in front. Whatever it was, the unsettling desire was exceptionally strong and took a concerted effort on my part to control it. It was something totally outside of my normal modes of thought.

We reached a room with two more beings in white outfits, and I was put into what seemed like a holding area. As I began to feel more aware of my surroundings, I started to panic. The stress was beyond belief! I began crying uncontrollably. I was about to ask them for help to calm me down, when one of the beings said something like, "Whoops, sorry," and suddenly I was calm. No drugs were involved. It's just some sort of conscious connection by which they can influence your mental state and calm you down.

Next, I went through a serious of painful medical procedures, some so painful that I couldn't stop myself from screaming in agony. After the first procedure, I remember asking the beings if there was anything I could do to help them. The question utterly confounded them; they were completely astonished that I might ask such a question after experiencing the procedure. As they moved to help me out of the room they seemed so dumbstruck I could have knocked them over with a feather. During the final medical procedure I had apparently lost consciousness. When I awoke, there were two aliens about 9 ½ feet tall, dressed in black uniforms, standing by the foot of the bed I lay on. To say that they were imposing would be putting it mildly. With them was another being, about 5 feet 2 inches tall and dressed in a beige outfit. Although I couldn't see any obviously female attributes, there was a strong sense that this being was female. In the most emotionless voice I've ever heard, she said, "We don't understand your anger." It was as if a mannequin had spoken.

At first, I didn't know what she was talking about. The whole time on the ship, from the decontamination chamber onward, I had been trying to cooperate and take part in the experience, asking them if I could help them and what it was they wanted. Then it hit me: *I had yelled at them.* The initial transport up to the ship had hurt, and I had lost control and yelled at them.

I turned my head away and tried to speak. What I wanted to say was, "I'm sorry, I just wasn't expecting it to hurt. I got angry because it hurt. I'm sorry." But I couldn't get it out. All I could manage was, "I'm sorry . . . ."

It was as if a veil had fallen away. She stepped forward and I was completely enveloped in an incredible sense of love and compassion. I tried to control myself, but the tears simply erupted from me and I cried. I clung to her and cried like a child. She said, "It's okay to cry. The strong ones cry."

After that, things get a little fuzzy. I know that we spoke at some length, but I cannot remember about what. The next clear memory I have is standing with her next to my car. It felt as though we had known each other for a very long time. We hugged and she said, "I wish I could stand beside you to face the things that you're going to have to face." And I said, "No, that's okay. I understand." In spite of the incredible feelings of love and connection, I knew that I couldn't stay there. My place wasn't there. I had to go. Several of the small beings were there as well, and the mood was joyful and loving mixed with a little hint of sadness. We said our farewells, and, as one of the smaller beings escorted me towards the car, I suddenly recalled my initial experience. I urgently jumped ahead of him and stretched for the door. It's okay, I said with a friendly smile that masked my relief . . . I'll get the door. I stepped back into the car's passenger seat.

Back on Terra Firma

The lights were moving away, the paralysis was gone. I don't recall screaming, but I do recall the sound of an echo of it. It was very odd. I kept my eyes closed, intending to count to ten, but after getting to about five, I opened my eyes. Around me lay the peaceful summer night with the irritating buzz of the mosquitoes in the air. There was nothing unusual. No lights in the sky, no people running around. The little truck stop and diner that I had pulled into earlier was still accepting its road-weary travellers.

I got out of the car. A transport truck had parked behind me, blocking the car from the view of anyone in the diner. I wondered if anyone coming or going might have seen something unusual. (Remember, at the time I didn't have access to the memories described above.) I checked my watch. It was after 3 A.M. and still dark. How much time had elapsed? I had no idea. Probably I should have been more upset. I was a little shaky but still relatively calm.

When I went into the diner everything seemed so . . . normal. The bright fluorescent lights washed out what little color was in the faces of the people who looked in my direction. There was no panic, no running around, and no excitement. It was just a peaceful little place in the middle of nowhere, with a few tired truckers and vacationers straining to stay awake.

In the cool restroom, I splashed warm water on my face and took a hard look in the mirror. Geez, I thought . . . the fluorescent lighting in here didn't compliment my pale skin any more than those guys in the diner. Other than looking like a person in desperate need of a blood transfusion I was completely normal. What now? Did anyone see anything? Should I even ask? Even though I had only fragmentary flashes of memory, I was determined to try and remember what had happened. Back in the diner, I cautiously approached the waitress and asked, "Excuse me miss . . . did you see anything outside?"

She said no, she hadn't. *The trucker*, I thought—what about the trucker who had parked beside me and blocked my car from view of the diner? He must have seen something! But when I looked out the window, my car was clearly visible outside. The trucker had gone!

"Honey," the waitress said, studying my face, "Were you looking for somebody?"

"Never mind," I mumbled, "They probably already left." What was I going to do—call the police and report this? Hardly. Besides, what could they possibly do?

"Oh," the waitress said, still eyeing me. "Do you want a coffee?"

After a short pause I said, yes, I would like a coffee. The thought of staying in that dark parking lot just gave me the creeps. In fact, getting the hell away from there suddenly seemed like a very good idea.

2

OVERVIEW OF PROOF

"There are more things in heaven and earth, Horatio,
Than are dreamt of in your philosophy."
—William Shakespeare

The goal of this book is not to convince anyone that the aliens are real. There are numerous articles, books, and websites devoted to that purpose. This book simply accepts that the aliens *are* real and proceeds from that perspective. However, because some readers may be unaware of the extensive documentation that is available, this chapter presents a very selective overview of the vast and growing collection of evidence that human beings are not alone in the universe.

Broadly speaking, there are three types of proof associated with extraterrestrial presence: observation of UFOs or other unusual phenomena; reports of direct contact and/or abduction; and after-the-fact physical proof, such as unexplained ground disturbances at sites where landings have been observed.

Taken as a whole, the body of proof is astounding. Many of the witnesses are highly credible people, including commercial pilots, astronauts, police officers, military officials, and well-respected scientists. Their reports are supplemented by the testimonies of literally thousands of other people who have seen UFOs or have had contact experiences.

It's always possible to find some way to question the credibility of any given individual, and undeniably, some contact reports are the by-product of either mental illness or conscious fakery. However, as increasing numbers of credible individuals come forward, it becomes ever harder to discount the collective truth of their experiences. A significant number of contactees have been evaluated by psychiatrists or psychologists and found to be free of mental disturbance, other than the post-traumatic stress that is fully consistent with the experiences they have reported. (Strictly speaking, the stress cannot be defined as "post-traumatic," since experiencers are fully aware that the event may not be over. The aliens may reappear at any time.)

Consider, for a moment, the list of skills that a human being must have in order to be considered a highly credible witness: excellent observational skills, discernment, and the ability to stay calm and focused in unusual situations. Our pilots, astronauts, police officers, and accredited scientists must surely rank high on this list. On any other matter, the testimony of such individuals would automatically be considered credible and taken seriously. With so many of these credible witnesses worldwide making reports of contact, we can be sure of one thing: *something* extraordinary is happening.

The contact process can be broken into six stages, as described in the rest of this chapter.

Stage One: Pre-1945

It's logical to assume that the aliens have been studying the Earth and human development for a very long time. We just don't know exactly when they became aware of us. It's plausible that we will never know.

In numerous cultures, there are historical references to strange beings and strange flying objects that have appeared in the sky. Some of these sightings have occurred at the locations of battles. I believe that as a result of our warlike nature, we've been under observation for some time. However, until World War II, these observations were conducted passively and from a distance, at least within the Western world.

Some people think that there's an extraterrestrial component to some ancient civilizations, but the best archaeological evidence suggests that the technologies in question were likely developed by humans alone. It's an issue that may, of course, never be fully settled. Likewise, there may be a long history of UFO abductions, but we won't know the full extent of the aliens' involvement with humanity unless they decide to tell us.

The aliens were prompted to change their approach from nonintrusive study to active intervention just prior to 1945. It was an era marked by the discovery of new nuclear technologies and a clear demonstration of humanity's unrestrained violence and aggression. Realizing that a full "take me to your leader" approach would never be in humanity's best long-term interests, the aliens opted instead to begin with a process of acclimation. In a marked departure from their earlier behavior, they began to allow frequent visual sightings of their craft. The purpose of this strategy was to slowly allow large numbers of people to become aware of, and accustomed to, their existence.

Within the military theater of operations, at least, the strategy was a success. During World War II, numerous anomalous objects, nicknamed "Foo-Fighters," were reported and photographed accompanying US bombers in the Pacific theater. John Spencer, who researched the phenomenon for his book *UFOs: The*

Definitive Casebook, states that these phenomena were definitely physical objects, not anomalous light sources. In some cases the objects took the form of small discs that flyers could actually feel clattering across the wings of their planes. After the war, it was determined that the Axis powers had encountered similar objects.

We do know that over the course of six years, from 1939 to 1945, more than $2 billion was spent on a very special initiative called the Manhattan Project. Some of the greatest minds of our time worked on refining uranium and putting together a working atomic bomb. Many of the scientists working on the development of this new weapon immediately recognized the consequences of what they had created and expressed remorse. Chief among the people who unleashed the power of the atom was Robert Oppenheimer, who oversaw the project from conception to completion. Upon observing the first successful atomic test, he uttered the prophetic words from the Hindu scripture. "Now I become death, the destroyer of worlds." The subsequent bombings of Hiroshima and Nagasaki marked the end of conventional warfare and the beginning of the age of nuclear war.

Stage Two: 1945 to 1960

"I can assure you that flying saucers, given that they exist, are not constructed by any power on earth."
—President Harry S. Truman, thirty-third president

In the middle of the 1940s, something changed the way the aliens were interacting with us. That something was the discovery, creation, and subsequent deployment of a new weapon of war.

At the time, no one made a connection between these foreign objects and the advent of the nuclear age. If anyone did think about an alien presence, it would have been to assume that the visits were prompted by an admiration for our shiny new technologies. No one suspected that the 'admiration' was in fact a growing alarm at humanity's increasing ability to use its shiny new toys to obliterate itself.

The aliens observed the increase in the imbalance between human spiritual development (our ability to live in peace) and our technological advancements during World War II, hence the move to an active intervention. The initial step of their strategy was highly successful. Asked about Foo Fighters, some World War II pilots would have had at least some knowledge of, if not personal experience of, the phenomenon. The process of contact had started.

The nuclear age changed our world. Nuclear weapons never brought long-lasting peace, but rather changed the way we fought our wars. Nuclear energy has held some promise for a cleaner fuel source and there are many examples of how this energy has been safely applied and been an environmental benefit. Of course it's not totally without risk—the Chernobyl reactor catastrophe, for example. It is, however, the proliferation of nuclear weapons capabilities in other countries that may pose the greater risk. As more and more countries (some of which are prone to factional violence) strive to develop nuclear capabilities, the future of the human race becomes correspondingly grim. Albert Einstein may have said it best. "The release of atomic energy has not created a new problem. It has merely made more urgent the necessity of solving an existing one."

Every new phenomenon has one defining moment. For UFOs, the moment came on June 24, 1947, when pilot Kenneth Arnold spotted a formation of nine unusual craft around Mount Rainier, Washington. Arnold subsequently described the movements of the objects as "like a saucer would if you skipped it across the water." Even though Arnold went on to describe the craft as "boomerang-shaped," the name *flying saucer* stuck.

As scientists began to study the flying saucer phenomenon, the more clinical term *unidentified flying object* was adopted. Although this phrase deliberately makes no inferences about what such objects might be, most people now consider the term to refer to space vehicles that are controlled by intelligent nonhuman beings.

In the years after 1947, there were many sightings, including sightings with multiple witnesses and sightings recorded on multiple radar-detection systems. Here is a very brief selection of credible sightings during that time:

July 1948: Eastern Airline pilots Captain C. Chiles and First Officer John Whitted, flying a DC-3 aircraft, reported a near-miss with a UFO. The object, estimated to be travelling at 500–700 mph, decelerated so rapidly to avoid collision that the DC-3 was violently shaken. No acceptable explanation for the incident was ever found.

October 1948: A pilot of the North Dakota Air National Guard, Second Lieutenant George Gorman, engaged an unknown craft in an aerial chase that lasted about thirty minutes. Air-traffic control visually confirmed the craft, which moved in patterns not considered possible for any known aircraft.

May 1950: The Trent family, farmers living near McMinnville, Oregon, photographed an unidentified craft flying over their farm. William Hartmann of The Condon Committee, a panel that investigated UFO activity, stated that the photographs were consistent with witness testimony: namely, that a silvery, disc-shaped flying object had flown past them. To date, studies of the photographs have not revealed any way in which the images, which are exceptionally clear, could possibly have been faked.

July 1952: On July 19, 1952, and again a week later, hundreds of people witnessed UFOs over Washington, DC. The objects were not only filmed, but were detected on three independent radar systems. For the most part, the objects travelled at 100 mph, but could accelerate to 7,000 mph. A Capital Airlines pilot, Captain S. Pierman, who was aloft during one of the sightings and confirmed the objects visually, stated, "These couldn't have been aircraft . . . they were moving too fast for that." Each time fighter jets were sent up to intercept, the objects disappeared, only to reappear after the fighters had left. The objects flew over the protected airspace of the Pentagon, the White House, and the Capitol Building. Although the official explanation was a "temperature inversion" (an atmospheric phenomenon), seasoned radar operators rejected the possibility as inconsistent with their experience.

December 1952: Captain John Harter and radar officer Lieutenant Sid Coleman, while flying a B-52 bomber back to their base after night training, spotted an object moving at more than 5,000 mph. Soon after, four UFOs were visible on all three of the plane's radar screens. Over the next few minutes, several UFOs flashed past the plane at high speeds, some pausing to pace the aircraft. The UFOs then pulled away and joined a much larger UFO, with which they appeared to dock or merge. The large craft then disappeared at a rate of about 9,000 mph.

Stage Three: 1960 to 1975

"We have, indeed, been contacted—perhaps even visited—by extraterrestrial beings, and the US government, in collusion with

the other national powers of the Earth, is determined to keep this
information from the general public."
—Victor Marchetti, former special assistant to the executive director of the CIA

Sometime in the early 1960s, the intervention moved into its next stage: direct contact. Bizarre accounts began to surface of small alien beings with large eyes who took people aboard spaceships and conducted intrusive medical procedures.

In North America, this period began with the experiences of Betty and Barney Hill, a married couple who lived in New Hampshire. In September 1961, while driving home from Montreal, Quebec, on US Highway 3, the Hills lost track of nearly two hours of time. Afterward, Barney suffered from insomnia and Betty had terrifying nightmares. After nearly two years of suffering, the Hills decided to see Boston psychiatrist Benjamin Simon. During separate hypnotic regressions, both Betty and Barney recounted that they had been abducted by small gray humanoid beings who performed detailed medical-like examinations centered on the Hills' reproductive systems. In spite of the fact that the Hills were hypnotized separately, Dr. Simon believed they were suffering from some sort of shared dream fantasy. However, the Hills persisted in their conviction that the events had actually happened. They had found physical traces of the experience on their car, and on the night of their experience, military radar had reported an unidentified flying object in the area.

In 1962, Admiral Roscoe Hillenkoetter, the first director of the CIA, made the following statement at a Washington press conference concerned with recent UFO sightings: "I know that neither Russia nor this country has anything even approaching such high speeds and maneuvers. Behind the scenes, high ranking officers are soberly concerned about the UFOs, but through official secrecy and ridicule, many citizens are led to believe that the unknown flying objects are nonsense."

US government documents substantiate the admiral's assertion. Under the Freedom of Information Act, UFO researcher Robert Hastings has uncovered numerous government documents confirming that, from the 1940s onward, the US military engaged in a deliberate disinformation campaign designed to convince the public that UFOs were not real. Hastings also uncovered documentation showing that by 1948 a US Air Force study of UFOs had concluded that the objects were interplanetary craft that were systematically observing the Earth. These government documents are now public record and can be reviewed by anyone who cares to see them (see appendix A).

The disinformation campaign included a gag order: the US Air Force ordered its personnel not to publicly discuss sightings. Around 1953, the Air Force issued a regulation called JANAP-146, which falls under espionage laws and prescribes severe penalties for reporting UFOs. The regulation was imposed not only on military pilots, but on civilian (airline) pilots as well. Understandably, public reporting by pilots and air-traffic personnel virtually stopped.

The sightings, however, did not. Based on reported UFO sightings made on radar by civilian or military air control, the objects' estimated speeds were commonly calculated at upwards of 6,000 miles per hour. To place this in perspective, on June 15, 2007, Reuters reported, "An experimental jet engine has been successfully tested at speeds of up to 11,000 km (6,835 miles) per hour, or 10 times the speed of sound, during trials in Australia's outback. . . ." Reuters noted that the jet's supersonic combustion engine, under joint development by Australian and American defense scientists, was limited to use in the thin upper layer of the atmosphere, far above the altitudes frequented by commercial aircraft. The logical question arises: if in the year 2007, cutting-edge human technology delivers an engine that attains over 6,000 miles per hour but must travel far above commercial aircraft to do so, then what were the objects seen by pilots and air-traffic controllers in the 1960s, 70s, and afterward, that were travelling at 6,000 mph in the lower atmosphere—and in many cases, executing abrupt changes of direction that the cutting-edge jet engine tested in 2007 is assuredly not capable of?

In summary, it appears that over the fifteen-year period from 1960 to 1975, there was an increase in the frequency of both sightings and contact episodes. Selected examples include:

April 1964: Near Soccoro, New Mexico, police officer Lonnie Zamura, responding to a blue light in the sky and believing it to be some kind of explosion, came upon a shiny object and, near it, two beings in white overalls. Zamura got out of his vehicle, only to witness the beings fly off in the object. Afterwards, the sand showed clear impressions and burn marks. Others saw the object in flight.

January 1967: In Ashburnham, Massachusetts, Betty Andreasson saw strange beings float into her house—through the walls. When the beings told her they needed food for their minds, Betty gave them a Bible. She went with them to their craft and underwent various examinations before being returned to her family. Much of the episode lay buried in her subconscious for about ten years, until she underwent regression therapy.

March 1967: Future UFO researcher Robert Hastings, then sixteen years of age and a self-confessed "air force brat," was spending time in the air-traffic control tower at the Maumstrom Air Force Base in Montana when he witnessed the controllers tracking five unidentified aerial targets. The objects were observed for about thirty minutes, during which time they hovered near the nuclear missile silos to the southeast of the base and performed high-speed aerial maneuvers. The air-traffic controllers were of the opinion that the objects were not helicopters or conventional aircraft. Two jets were scrambled to intercept, but the objects eluded them by ascending at an extreme rate of speed. Under the Freedom of Information Act, Hastings has since uncovered US Air Force documents that reveal literally dozens of similar sightings around military and nuclear installations, including numerous sightings made by facility personnel over nuclear power plants and missile defense facilities.

December 1967: In Ashland, Nebraska, patrolman Herb Schirmer investigated a flying saucer and was taken onto the craft. The entities wore uniforms with an emblem of a winged serpent and mentioned a breeding analysis program.

1971: Christina and Stanislaf Grof published a book titled *The Stormy Search for Self.* While not primarily about UFO encounters, the book was a milestone because it was one of the earliest books to suggest that UFO encounters may have a significant spiritual component.

1974: Dr. Paul R. Hill, an aeronautic scientist, completed a manuscript titled *Unconventional Flying Objects.* Dr. Hill had worked at the Langley Research Center under NACA (The National Advisory Committee for Aeronautics) and NASA from 1939 to 1970, after which he retired with an Exceptional Service Medal. In the manuscript, discovered by his daughter after his death, Hill documented his years of exposure to UFOs during the course of his work. In 1952, Hill was forbidden by NASA to publicly communicate in any way that NASA was interested in UFOs. However, he kept notes of his sightings and the experiments he made during his career, and developed theories about how the craft might function. Based on his personal sightings, Dr. Hill, who was an aeronautics specialist, realized that the technology he was seeing was beyond the capabilities of human beings. The book was published in 1995 by Hampton Roads Publishing Company.

November 1975: Travis Walton was one of a seven-man team cutting trees in Sitgraves National Park in Arizona. One day, when the group was on its way out of the woods at the end of the workday, they saw a large gold UFO hovering in the air. All seven men saw the object, which they described as having windows and being saucer-shaped with a dome on top. Inexplicably, Travis Walton got out of his vehicle and ran toward the object, which emitted a ray of bluish light that struck him. The other men fled. Several days later, Travis Walton reappeared and said he had been abducted. All but one of the men, including Walton, took polygraph tests and were judged to be telling the truth. The seventh man was reported as being too upset to be tested.

Please Be Advised That There *Is* a Santa Claus: The Space Program

The space programs in both Russia and the USA have yielded ample evidence that UFOs are real. Only a small sample of the evidence derived from the US space program is summarized in this section.

The *Mercury* Astronauts

DONALD SLAYTON

Donald Slayton, a test pilot who later became a *Mercury* astronaut, publicly described a UFO encounter he had in 1951:

"I was testing a P-51 fighter in Minneapolis when I spotted this object. I was at about 10,000 feet on a nice, bright, sunny afternoon. I thought the object was a kite, then I realized that no kite is gonna fly that high. As I got closer, it looked like a weather balloon, gray and about three feet in diameter. But as soon as I got behind the darn thing it didn't look like a balloon anymore. It looked like a saucer, a disc. About the same time, I realized that it was suddenly going away from me—and there I was, running at about 300 miles per hour. I tracked it for a little way, and then all of a sudden the damn thing just took off. It pulled about a 45 degree climbing turn and accelerated, and just flat disappeared."

JOSEPH A. WALKER

NASA pilot/astronaut Joseph Walker has stated that one of his tasks was to detect UFOs during his X-15 flights. In April, 1962, he filmed five or six UFOs during a fifty-mile-high flight, the second time he had filmed UFOs during his flights.

SCOTT CARPENTER

Scott Carpenter flew the second American manned orbital flight, *Aurora 7*, on May 24, 1962. He later assumed NASA duties as executive assistant to the director of the Manned Spaceflight Center. He has been quoted as saying, "At no time when the astronauts were in space were they alone: there was a constant surveillance by UFOs."

GORDON COOPER

Gordon Cooper, one of the later *Mercury* astronauts, sighted numerous UFOs during his career. In 1951, while piloting an F-86 Sabrejet over Germany, Cooper saw metallic, saucer-shaped discs flying at high altitudes. The craft could outmaneuver all the American fighter planes. Of this and other episodes, Cooper later testified before the United Nations: "I did have occasion in 1951 to have two days of observation of many flights of them, of different sizes, flying in fighter formation, generally from east to west over Europe." Cooper testified that one of the other astronauts had actually witnessed a UFO on the ground. He also stated, "I believe that these extraterrestrial vehicles and their crews are visiting this planet from other planets . . . Most astronauts were reluctant to discuss UFOs."

In 1963, Cooper went into space in a *Mercury* capsule. During the capsule's final orbit of Earth, Cooper reported making visual contact with a glowing, greenish object that was quickly approaching the *Mercury* capsule. The UFO was picked up by the ground-tracking station's radar, indicating that it was not some sort of light phenomenon or mirage, but a solid object. The UFO sighting was reported by the news media, but when Cooper landed, reporters were told they could not ask him about the object.

In a later interview taped by J. L. Ferrando, Major Cooper described an incident in Florida, during which "I saw with my own eyes a defined area of ground being consumed by flames, with four indentations left by a flying object which had descended in the middle of a field. Beings had left the craft (there were other traces to prove this). They seemed to have studied topography, they had collected soil samples, and, eventually, they returned to where they had come from, disappearing at enormous speed . . . I happen to know that authority did just about everything to keep this incident from the press and TV, in fear of a panicky reaction from the public."

Major Cooper also stated that "I can now reveal that every day, in the USA, our radar instruments capture objects of form and composition unknown to us. And there are thousands of witness reports and a quantity of documents to prove this, but nobody wants to make them public. Why? Because authority is afraid that people may think of God-knows-what kind of horrible invaders. So the password still is: 'We have to avoid panic by all means.'"

Gordon Cooper wrote a book titled *Leap of Faith: An Astronaut's Journey into the Unknown*, which included information on his UFO experiences and the systematic military and government coverup of UFO activities.

The *Gemini* Astronauts

ED WHITE AND JAMES MCDIVITT

In June 1965, while passing over Hawaii in a *Gemini* space capsule, astronauts Ed White and James McDivitt spotted a strange-looking metal object that had long arms sticking out of it. McDivitt took photographs, but they have never been publicly released.

FRANK BORMAN

During his and James Lovell's *Gemini* flight in December 1965, astronaut Frank Borman reported seeing a UFO. In the publicly heard transmission, *Gemini* control at Cape Kennedy asked Borman if the object might be the booster rocket that had been jettisoned from their own craft. Lovell confirmed that he had the booster in view, and the object he was seeing was something different.

The *Apollo* Astronauts

JAMES LOVELL

On Christmas Day 1968, after *Apollo 8* emerged from its orbit behind the moon, James Lovell announced, "Please be informed that there is a Santa Claus."

Innocuous words? Perhaps not; Maurice Chatelain, former chief of NASA Communications Systems, has since explained that, to the best of his recollection, Walter Schirra on *Mercury 8* was the first astronaut, but by no means the last, to use the code phrase "Santa Claus" to indicate the presence of a UFO near a space capsule. Chatelain also explained that all astronauts were under strict orders not to reveal any information about the flying saucers. Perhaps Lovell just couldn't resist.

NEIL ARMSTRONG AND EDWIN "BUZZ" ALDRIN

Shortly after Neil Armstrong and Edwin "Buzz" Aldrin made their historic *Apollo 11* moon landing on July 21, 1969, one of the astronauts referred to a "light" in or near a crater on the moon's surface. After mission control requested further information, nothing more was heard on the television transmission. However, Otto Binder, a former NASA employee, states that unnamed radio hams with their own VHF receivers picked up the following exchange, which was not heard on television:

> NASA: What's there? Mission Control calling *Apollo 11* . . .
> *Apollo 11:* These "babies" are huge, sir! Enormous! Oh my god! You wouldn't believe it! I'm telling you there are other spacecraft out there, lined up on the far side of the crater edge! They're on the moon watching us!

Later, during a NASA symposium, Neil Armstrong was asked what had really happened on the moon. Armstrong stated that, although he could not go into details, they had been "warned off" by the aliens, who had made it clear there would be no space station or city built on the moon. Armstrong is quoted as saying, ". . . their ships were far superior to ours both in size and technology. Boy, were they big! . . . and menacing! No, there is no question of a space station."

This version of events is substantiated by Dr. Vladimir Azhazha, a physicist and professor of mathematics at Moscow University, who is quoted as saying, "Neil Armstrong relayed the message to Mission Control that two large, mysterious objects were watching them after having landed near the moon module. But this message was never heard by the public—because NASA censored it."

Interestingly enough, NASA now implements a five-minute delay on all "live" transmissions from space; even if the TV transmission says "live" coverage, it is on a five-minute delay. NASA needs that editing capability!

COMMANDER EUGENE CERNAN

In a 1973 *Los Angeles Times* article, Eugene Cernan, commander of *Apollo 17,* was quoted as saying, "I've been asked [about UFOs] and I've said publicly I thought they [UFOs] were somebody else, some other civilization."

Stage Four: 1975 to 1990

"I don't laugh at people anymore when they say they've seen UFOs. I've seen one myself."
—President Jimmy Carter

This stage of the emerging contact phenomenon was characterized by the first attempts to systematically research, document, and interpret the meanings of abductees' stories. Hints begin to emerge that there was a spiritual component to the abduction experiences. The abductions and interactions themselves became much more complex. A selective chronology of the period is as follows:

November 1980: British constable Alan Godfrey sighted a dome-shaped object hovering over the road. The object was about twenty feet wide and had windows. Hypnotic regression later revealed that Godfrey believed he had been taken aboard the craft and examined.

1981: UFO researcher Budd Hopkins published a book entitled *Missing Time,* in which he reported his work with abductees. In the book, Hopkins described some emerging patterns of physical phenomena associated with the abduction experience: cuts, body marks, scoop marks, and implanted foreign objects. Hopkins's second book, *Intruders,* released in 1987, discussed the sexual and reproductive aspects of the experiences.

1987: Whitley Strieber published the bestseller *Communion,* a firsthand account of his abduction experiences and subsequent attempts to come to terms with those experiences.

Stage Five: 1990 to 2005

"The evidence is overwhelming that planet Earth is being visited by intelligently controlled extraterrestrial spacecraft. . . . The greater the education, the more likely a person is to accept this proposition."
—Dr. Stanton Friedman, former defense contractor and nuclear physicist

During this time period, the number of sightings continued to increase, particularly over heavily populated areas. This contrasted with the tendency of early sightings to occur in remote areas. By this time, an increasing number of credible individuals had become involved in UFO and abduction research and had begun to publicly report their findings.

DR. JOHN MACK

Perhaps the most notable was Dr. John Mack, a Pulitzer Prize-winning psychiatrist from Harvard University. Mack, who was introduced to the field by Budd Hopkins, initially approached the phenomenon with a belief that it was some sort of new or emerging psychosis or disturbance state. However, he ultimately concluded that the vast majority of the abductees he had interviewed were psychologically healthy individuals simply trying to contend with real, extraordinary experiences. Mack reported that, during hypnotic regression, abductees experienced such intensely powerful emotions that even a determined skeptic would find it hard to deny that *something* extraordinary and emotionally shattering had taken place.

Mack identified cases of the abduction phenomenon among Native Americans, and in South Africa, Brazil, and Malaysia. He considered abduction experiences to be a worldwide phenomenon, writing, "People of sound mind, hundreds of thousands if not millions of people from all over the world, not just in the Western countries, but on other continents and among indigenous people, are having what seem like authentic, incontrovertible encounters with some sort of beings that apparently enter into our physical world and communicate to us about ourselves, and seem in some way to be connecting with us."

Mack also shattered the misconception that people who report abduction experiences do it because they crave the limelight. On the contrary, he reported, some abductees go to great lengths to remain anonymous. Of such people, the *Forbidden Science* website has written, "Rather than trying to convince people that the abduction is a real event, they seek therapy in hopes of uncovering a treatable mental illness. Studies have also been conducted by psychologists to determine whether or not abductees exhibit a high degree of certain personality traits such as fantasy proneness; the results, however, showed that most abductees fall within the normal range."

In 1994, John Mack published his first book, *Abduction*, in which he wrote:

> I was dealing with a phenomenon that I felt could not be explained psychiatrically, yet was simply not possible within the framework of the Western scientific worldview. My choices then were either to stretch and twist psychology beyond reasonable limits, overlooking aspects of the phenomenon that could not be explained psychologically . . . or I might open to the possibility that our consensus framework of reality is too limited and that . . . a new scientific paradigm might be necessary in order to understand what was going on.

After Dr. Mack published *Abduction*, Harvard Medical School appointed a special faculty committee to review his clinical care and clinical investigations related to his work with abductees. In response, Dr. Bruce Cornet, a highly accomplished geologist and paleobotanist on the Harvard faculty, wrote the committee in Mack's defense. Part of Dr. Cornet's letter reads as follows:

> With regard to the issue of extraterrestrial intelligence, it is my professional and academic judgment that there are ample physical, geophysical, and photographic data collected by me during my two and a half years of research into the UFO phenomenon to support the hypothesis that this planet is currently inhabited by more than one sentient intelligent humanoid species, and that this non-human species has in its possession technologies thousands of years beyond our own.

Dr. Cornet's scientific investigations are treated in detail in chapter 8. After a fifteen-month process, Harvard's special faculty committee took no disciplinary action and affirmed that Dr. Mack was in no way limited in his choice of future research.

In 1999, Dr. Mack wrote his second book, *Passport to the Cosmos*, in which he expanded on his original ideas. He also founded Harvard's Program for Extraordinary Experience Research (PEER). After conducting research in various countries, PEER concluded that people throughout the world are experiencing alien abductions that are in some ways similar to the accounts reported in the United States. However, the abductions also appear to have distinct cultural differences, depending on how each culture frames its experiences.

Worldwide Sightings

MEXICO

In the summer of 1991, thousands of people saw swarms of UFOs over Mexico City. Despite the fact that numerous videos and photos were taken, the event barely made the news in the rest of North America or overseas.

Since that time, there have been numerous mass sightings over Mexico City. One of the most recent occurred on June 30, 2005. Again, there were multiple witnesses, and multiple videotapes were taken. The tapes showed a number of silver spheres moving through the sky in perfect formation. Subsequent analysis of the videotapes has confirmed that the objects were not weather balloons, which, in any case, do not move in perfect synchronization.

EUROPE

Sightings and encounters have been reported in virtually every country in Europe. Witnesses include civil and military pilots. Many of these sightings have been confirmed by multiple witnesses, including air-traffic control personnel. For example, in one 1976 sighting off Portugal, the pilots of three different commercial aircraft all confirmed the presence of a UFO, which was described by one witness as a silver object surrounded by bright light. Based on the radar trace, the captain of one aircraft estimated the object to be about three times the size of a 200,000-ton tanker.

For detailed descriptions of many reliable sightings throughout Europe, see John Spencer's book, *UFOs: The Definitive Casebook.*

FRANCE

In June 1999, high-level French officials published a study titled (in English translation) *UFOs and Defense: What Must We Be Prepared For?* The report, a comprehensive assessment of the UFO phenomenon, was authored by COMETA, a French committee of former members of the French Institute for Advanced National Defense Studies. Those involved in the study included General Norlain, a former commander of the French Tactical Air Force and military counsellor to the prime minister of France; General Denis Letty, an air force fighter pilot; and Andre Lebeau, former head of the National Center for Space Studies, the French equivalent of NASA.

The COMETA report states: "The number of sightings that are completely unexplained, despite the abundance and quality of data, is growing throughout the world." Regarding the hypothesis that extraterrestrials exist, the report concluded: "Strong presumptions exist in its favor, and if correct, it is loaded with significant consequences."

The COMETA report is a significant document because it confirms the fact that high-quality sightings (sightings that are difficult, if not impossible, to dispute or explain away within a normal frame of reference) are increasing in number. Further evidence from the study suggests that the characteristics of this phenomenon are changing in a way that may well have direct ramifications for our generation.

USSR

"Unidentified flying objects are a very serious subject which we must study fully. We appeal to all viewers to send us details of strange flying craft seen over territories of the Soviet Union. This is a serious challenge to science and we need the help of all Soviet citizens."
—Professor Felix Zigel, Moscow Aviation Institute

USSR was the site of innumerable UFO sightings and contact reports. Here are two involving military sites and/or aircraft:

In 1982, two UFOs were observed at the Baikonur Space Center. Afterward, personnel discovered extensive damage to a launch pad and nearby building.

In 1990, during test flights of an Aeroflot IL-96-300 plane at Moscow airport, several strange objects were seen in the sky and photographed.

OTHER COUNTRIES

In September 1976, two Iranian Air Force pilots flying F-4s encountered a UFO north of Tehran. The radar indicated an object the size of a 707 tanker (about the size of a Boeing 707). The object was very bright, with blue, red, green, and orange strobe lights that flashed in such rapid sequence that they were all visible simultaneously. As the F-4 pursued the object, a smaller object emerged from the main object and approached the F-4. The F-4 pilot tried to fire a missile, but his weapons control panel failed, and he lost communications. When he took evasive action, the pursuing object rejoined the main unknown object.

Afterward, the pilot's night vision was impaired by the brightness of the UFO to the point that he had to land using instruments.

In November 1986, Japan Air Lines Flight 1628 was enroute from France to Japan via Anchorage, Alaska, when it was paced at 39,000 feet by an unidentified craft that the captain, Kenju Terauchi, described as about twice as big as an aircraft carrier. The object accompanied the plane for half an hour and was detected on radar by air-traffic control.

Numerous compilations of sightings in China have been published. These include reports by military personnel and descriptions of a 1977 mass sighting, during which more than 300 people saw two glowing orange craft that descended so low over the crowd of witnesses that witnesses could feel the heat produced by the objects.

It appears that the Chinese government is taking an active interest in the UFO phenomenon, but this is difficult to confirm. As world dynamics change and China becomes more of a superpower, as it explores space more aggressively, it will be interesting to see whether that country follows the North American approach of denial and coverup, or whether the Chinese government will claim the great prize of having "discovered" extraterrestrial life. In historic terms, it would be a very tempting prize.

Physical Proof

"The evidence that there are objects which have been seen in our atmosphere, and even on terra firma, that cannot be accounted for either as manmade objects or as any physical force or effect known to our scientists seems to me to be overwhelming."
—Lord Hill-Norton, chief of defense staff, Ministry of Defense, Great Britain

Physical evidence can be difficult to obtain, in part because the military organizations charged with investigating extraterrestrial phenomena tend to be very secrecy-oriented. Anyone interested in reading more about physical proof is referred to John Spencer's book *UFOs: The Definitive Casebook.* However, a few general remarks are in order here.

There is physical evidence of UFOs. This has occurred when they have landed and left behind physical traces on the ground. In other cases, such physical evidence of extraterrestrials may be explained in ways that don't involve extraterrestrials at all. Sometimes the causes are unclear or open to interpretation. This shouldn't be surprising. Consider a typical criminal trial. For every expert witness who interprets the physical evidence in one way, it's usually possible to dig up another expert who will cast aspersions on the first expert's testimony. Every day, our courts convict based on their belief that Expert A's conclusions make more sense than Expert B's.

Using this system, we pass judgment on human lives—and yet, we somehow expect that every case of extraterrestrial contact must yield completely unambiguous physical evidence in order to be credible. Human criminal courts are not held to that standard! In legal proceedings, physical evidence is only one of a number of relevant factors, and so it should be with UFO sightings. There have been many extraterrestrial sightings in which the physical evidence has not only been inexplicable by "regular" means, but has fully corroborated the eyewitness accounts of highly trustworthy individuals like police officers. The burden of proof has been met. Clearly, if a person confronted with this kind of evidence is unwilling to at least acknowledge the *possibility* of an extraterrestrial presence, then what we're dealing with is not a reasoning mind, but a closed one.

Stage Six: 2005 to 2020

[Regarding evidence of an extraterrestrial presence]
"As far as I'm concerned, it's irrefutable."
—Paul Hellyer, former Canadian minister of defense

It's unlikely this will be the final stage of the UFO phenomenon, but it will arguably be one of the most interesting. For reasons explained later in this book, I believe that the number of sightings over heavily populated areas will continue to increase, and the number of people reporting contact or abduction experiences will increase as well. Some governments will finally acknowledge the reality of the phenomenon and begin to implement policies to deal with the public desire for more information. The real challenge in this stage is to prepare ourselves to cope with the impending changes in our lives.

There is also a report coming out of the Carnegie Institution for Science in Washington, DC, that there may not be just one planet out there somewhere that is capable of creating and sustaining life, but as many as 10 billion trillion planets.

The previous information is only a very selective sample of the credible reports that are available. Those wishing to know more are referred to Websites and Recommended Reading in appendix A.

I don't believe that it's my job to prove the existence of UFOs. There are many people in a much better position than I to do that. My purpose in this book is to explain what's likely to happen and why, then discuss the things that we can do to prepare for the inevitable.

3

INTERVENTION

"As we acquire more knowledge, things do not become more comprehensible, but more mysterious."
—Albert Schweitzer

Intervention. That's the word that best fits what the aliens are here to do. The relationship they're creating with humanity is, first and foremost, an intervention. The following chapters will describe the elements of this intervention and explain why it's taking place.

Very briefly, there are five basic elements to the abduction phenomenon. Psychiatrist John Mack was the first to identify these elements, which are:

Medical Procedures: Contactees undergo a variety of procedures, including physical examination and other procedures that appear to indicate a direct intervention in the physical functioning of the individual. Much of the aliens' interest seems to focus on the central nervous system and the reproductive systems of both men and women.

Information about Protecting Humanity and the Earth: Contactees are often shown images, either on television monitors or by telepathic means, of the Earth undergoing various types of catastrophe. Common themes involve environmental disaster and the Earth's destruction via nuclear weapons.

Transformation and Spirituality: As contactees deal with their fear and begin to assimilate their experiences, they tend to develop a strong sense of spirituality and spiritual growth.

Relationships: Central to the phenomenon are the powerful relationships that develop between the abductee and one or more alien beings. The beings have consistently demonstrated a desire to develop deep and lasting bonds with their human contactees.

Alien Hybrid Program: Some female contactees report experiences in which they are impregnated with fetuses that are later removed before being carried to term. Male contactees may have sperm samples taken. Some of these people report that in later abductions, they are shown hybrid offspring and told that the offspring are genetically their children.

Before discussing these specific aspects of the contact phenomenon, it's useful to make a general assessment of the overall patterns involved in contact. Assuming the extraterrestrial aliens are intelligent and have a purpose, the patterns behind their actions should let us reconstruct (or at least speculate intelligently upon) those purposes. Once we understand why the aliens are doing what they're doing, we can respond appropriately, both to the aliens and to the human beings who are having contact experiences and struggling to assimilate them. Ultimately, humans and aliens may be able to help one another, but one thing is clear: if we hope to become active participants in whatever is transpiring, our first step must be to try and understand the phenomenon.

In attempting to reconstruct the aliens' motives, my general scientific education and career in health and safety and occupational hygiene have been invaluable. Science in general, and accident/incident investigations in particular, focus on the use of empirical/rational methods to investigate environments and events, evaluate risks, establish causes, and develop strategies for change. Much of my work involves understanding human behavior, because unless you understand why people act the way they do, attempts to change their behavior are likely to fail. This professional training and experience in assessing human behaviors have been very helpful in developing an understanding of what the aliens are doing, and why.

One obstacle to uncovering the full meaning of the UFO phenomenon is that every person will tend to evaluate the events based on his or her social and cultural perspectives. I'm no exception; my observations will be colored by my own social and cultural norms. It may not be possible for me to have a deep understanding of what the UFO phenomenon means to people of different religious and cultural backgrounds. All the better reason for us to encourage worldwide exploration of the UFO phenomenon and its meanings to other societies!

Why Are They Here?

Some assume that the extraterrestrials are interested in us because humanity has finally developed the technological capacity to reach for the stars. A superficially reasonable assumption—but dead wrong.

The aliens are here because humanity is in danger of using

its technology to annihilate itself. Their goal is not technological, but spiritual; they want to motivate us to make some crucial changes in the way we interact with the Earth and one another.

As discussed in chapter 2, the UFO phenomenon really started to develop in the Pacific theater during World War II—the war in which the first nuclear bomb was dropped. Some people have asserted that the German development of U2 rockets showed the capacity to eventually take humanity into space, and that's why the extraterrestrials became interested. Again, this is incorrect. The U2 rockets were not carrying peace missions into space; they were serving as massive weapons platforms for exterminating other human beings.

As nuclear technology developed, UFO sightings around nuclear installations and air bases became relatively common. From this, we can infer that the UFO phenomenon is tied to human conflict and potentially destructive technologies, not to technological advancement per se. The aliens have been watching us for some time, hoping that we might set ourselves on the right path. In fact, they appear to have followed the classic pattern used by the United Nations in monitoring areas of potential conflict: first send observers, then, if necessary, intervene. When the first nuclear weapons were used in World War II, the observation phase ended and the intervention phase began.

Within the social sciences, the word *intervention* has a very specific meaning. Typically, interventions are made without the consent of the individuals in question in order to protect them from the consequences of their own destructive behaviors. An authority figure makes a decision, and the results are forced upon the individual. You *will* go into rehab. You *will* be under house arrest. You *will* undergo mandatory counseling. Interventions can be carried out with love and kindness, but at their root there is usually an underlying element of sternness, and certainly an element of force. Activities are imposed on the individual for the ultimate good of the individual and society.

In the simplest possible terms, the human race has been placed in rehab. The aliens have decided that, if left to ourselves, we will annihilate ourselves and most every living thing on Earth. As a result, they have initiated an intervention to change the course of human behavior. It's not clear how many alien species are involved, but at least one nonhuman species has chosen to interact with human beings to assist us through this difficult stage in our development.

I don't want to suggest that this intervention is a simple mercy mission. It's very possible that the aliens see something in us that is unique and so special that it's worth saving. Maybe the universe will need us in the future. Whether their motives are purely altruistic, or their future and fate are somehow intertwined with ours, is not clear. Humanity may have a role that extends well beyond this space/time system and into the millennia to follow. Regardless of what the future holds, our most immediate challenges are here in the present.

How Long Have They Been Here?

"It is my conclusion that UFOs do exist, are very real, and are spaceships from another or more than one solar system. They are possibly manned by intelligent observers who are members of a race carrying out long-range scientific investigations of our earth for centuries."
—Professor Hermann Oberth, father of modern rocketry
Published in *UFO News* in 1974 and quoted in the *Above Top Secret* website

No one really knows exactly how long the aliens have been here. Throughout history there have been hundreds of accounts of strange objects being seen in the sky. In 216 B.C. in Sardinia, soldiers reported seeing shiplike objects in the sky and having their weapons burst into flames in their hands. In 1566, in Basel, Germany, fleets of huge globes were seen in the sky above the town. In 1897, Alexander Hamilton, a former member of the US House of Representatives, filed an affidavit stating that he, his son, and a farmhand had watched a large cigar-shaped object glide to rest in a field about 200 yards from his home. On the underside of the object was a cabin that appeared to be made of glass; inside were six occupants that Hamilton described as the strangest beings he had ever seen. People who had known Hamilton for over thirty years filed written affidavits stating that they had never heard his word questioned and that they believe his statement to be true and correct.

Many cultures have legends that involve aliens from the sky. And of course Christianity speaks of angels. Are the angels referred to in the Bible in fact aliens? (If so, I can only hope that swearing at angels falls within the category of forgivable sins.) Is it possible that the star of Bethlehem was a UFO attempting to draw attention to the birth of Jesus, who was destined to be a spiritual leader? We can only speculate. However, it may be interesting to reflect on these modern-day definitions of angels.

"Angels are intelligent beings, capable of feelings, yet a different species who have their existence on a slightly finer vibrational frequency from the one to which our physical senses are tuned."
—Ask Your Angels, by Alma Daniel, Timothy Wyllie, and Andrew Ramer

"The primary significance of angels lies not in who or what they are, but rather what they do. Their inherent nature cannot be separated from their relationship with the Prime Mover, the God or Ultimate Source."
—Angels: An Endangered Species, by Malcolm Godwin

Whether or not the aliens are the angels described in various religions, we can be relatively sure that they've been here for a long time. The ones that I've encountered all speak English fluently with no accent, and that takes time. Our language is heavily influenced by our cultural experiences; even brilliant linguists need time to learn the vernacular. The aliens may be more advanced than we are in many ways, but they're not gods. Yet there is no reason to believe that they haven't already mastered most of the languages of humanity. The lack of a discernable accent suggests to me that they may have organized themselves into subgroups responsible for dealing with human beings from a specific geographical and cultural location. There are numerous benefits to organizing contact in this fashion.

Another reason to believe that the aliens have been here for some time is that they appear to have a very thorough understanding of our social systems, including marriage. On our wedding night, they paid my wife and me a special visit, and although the details remain private, I'm convinced that this shared experience and the bond of understanding it created between us was their wedding gift. (As of this writing, we've been married eighteen years and counting.) I would have to consider it as one of the most unusual wedding gifts anyone has received. No worries about repacking that one.

Yet another argument for the long-term presence of the aliens involves the interior architecture of their ships. Much of the ship that I observed was designed and built to the anthropometric needs of human beings and not the aliens themselves. The temperature, lighting, and humidity were also completely consistent with comfort levels for human beings. (Later in the book I'll discuss additional proof that illustrates the ship was designed to hold many contactees at a time.) Consider the effort they must have made to adapt their own biology to exist in an environment that would be comfortable for us. This kind of strategic planning, engineering excellence, and an extraordinary commitment of vast resources argue for a long-term relationship.

Are They "Real"?

"UFOs are as real as the airplanes that fly over your head."
—Paul Hellyer, former Canadian minister of defense 1963–1967

Some researchers have avoided committing themselves to a belief that the contact experiences are physically real. Instead, they suggest that because so many manifestations of the encounters are psychological, the experiences might be purely mental phenomena (real, but exclusively mental), in which nothing really happens "out there" in physical reality.

In my experience, this is not correct. There is a definite physical component to the experiences. The abduction experience does not take place purely within the contactee's head; it also takes place within objective physical reality. In fact, that is one aspect of the encounters that the beings wanted me to remember: physical reality *is* involved.

One reason that researchers who aren't contactees may misinterpret the experience is that contact involves a direct union of consciousness—a meeting of minds, if you will—that is far more intimate than any human encounter. Humans react on physical cues (like facial expressions, body language, and scent), and on verbal cues, but even in the deepest human love, we do not experience the fusion of consciousness that is characteristic of these contact experiences. The aliens have the ability to literally reach out with their consciousness and connect to the human psyche. They touch our minds and souls in the same way that humans touch one another's bodies. Because this is such an uncharacteristic experience for us, some researchers have interpreted it to mean that contact is not a physical experience, but occurs on a purely mental plane. This is untrue. The physical plane may or may not be involved, depending on the aliens' purposes.

For example, when the being contacted me while I was meditating, it was a nonphysical experience. The being never physically entered the room; the only contact in that case was a meeting of consciousnesses. By contrast, the Winnipeg abduction experience was both physical and mental. In other words, it "really happened" in the physical plane. I was physically taken to another location and underwent physical experiences, during which a meeting of consciousnesses also took place.

What Do They Look Like?

It's important to remember that I have only had experience with one group of alien beings. We have no idea how many more may be involved. One could assume that if there is one species visiting us then we should not be surprised to find others. Reports from people who have seen markedly different looking aliens have been made. The dramatic variations in the design of some UFOs also suggest different species are involved. Yet I must confess that despite recalling their images through hypnosis and also seeing them while in full waking consciousness, I am not sure exactly what they look like. (Perplexed? So was I, at first.)

After the Winnipeg encounter, I tried to understand my experiences by searching for accounts made by other people who I thought were highly credible, and trying to relate their experiences to mine. Because my science background had taught me that if you rely on bad data, you get incorrect conclusions, I worked very hard to find and concentrate on the experiences of one or two people whose accounts seemed highly credible.

One of these people was Whitley Strieber. Strieber reported interacting with beings about 3 ½ feet tall, with large, coal-black eyes that had no pupils. The description fit the aliens I'd seen, except for the eyes. Instead of seeing beings with the totally black, almost insect-like eyes that Strieber had reported, I saw beings with a human eye structure (pupil, iris, etc.) that had large blue pupils. These eyes were three or four times the size of human eyes, but the structure itself was similar. It was a mystery. I knew what I'd seen and was confident that Strieber knew what he'd seen, and it all correlated except for that one point of difference: the eyes. If different eye colors were possible, I had to wonder why this particular group *all* had blue eyes, with no color differentiation. It suggested a gene pool that was either extraordinarily shallow or tightly controlled.

Another puzzling thing was that even though the beings I observed all had the human eye structure, the eyes *did not move within their sockets* the way human eyes do. It was downright strange: an eye structure based on a pupil, when combined with a visual system based on the coordinated focusing of two eyes, should require the eyes to be able to move independently of the head. Yet I was sure that the aliens' eyes had never moved in their sockets. It didn't make sense. Why evolve a specific type of visual system, but not the capacity to use it? I was sure these were the same beings that Strieber had seen. Why, then, was everything the same except for the eyes?

There was only one answer that made sense: we were both seeing the same species, we were just seeing them differently. It's not clear whether the beings actually had the ability to change form, or whether I was simply perceiving them differently, but either way, *I was seeing what I needed to see.* During the initial abduction, I had kept my eyes shut for fear of losing control. Had they perceived my fear and tried to make themselves more familiar, less terrifying? Because they can communicate directly between consciousnesses, as well as verbally, they can pick up our thoughts and fears quite easily. Had they picked up on mine? *(Geez, Jim really gets upset when he sees us. Maybe if we show him blue eyes it'll be a little less threatening.)*

In retrospect, because of what followed, I believe this is true. I believe that the blue eyes were their attempt to soften my experience with them. Whether they had actually made alterations to their physical appearance or had simply altered the way I perceived them, they made sure that I saw what I needed to see. This sort of behavior would go a long way toward explaining why a variety of "archetypal" appearances have been described for the aliens, the small-statured, large-headed beings being only one of them. Perhaps the archetypes correlate to different sociocultural backgrounds, with the aliens taking care to appear in the most appropriate form for each cultural group. For example, many Russian sightings involve large humanoid beings eight or nine feet tall, a rather heroic archetype that fits well with the Russian psyche.

Even if the aliens can change their outward appearance, the physical structures they choose to adopt must still be functional. The prevalence of large pupils, and the other eye structures that have been reported by others, suggest that the eyes have adapted for a dimly lit environment. Maybe their visual perception extends well beyond the visible light electromagnetic spectrum of our species. Given that the interior of the ship was bright (I would estimate a brightness of more than 1,000 lux), the eye adaptation appears to be for another environment not associated with the craft . . . perhaps for abducting people at night when they will least be missed?

Why Abduct People, *Anyway?*

Logistically speaking, it would be much less complicated for the aliens to do their work within the contactee's own environment—in other words, to *not* transport contactees to another location. Because transport *is* occurring, it's reasonable to assume there are practical reasons for temporarily relocating the contactee to a more controlled environment.

Privacy may be a consideration. It's reasonable to assume that in the early stages of an intervention, the aliens may want to keep the contacts private, especially if they have any knowledge of the way that our society tends to ridicule contactees. It's a sobering thought that the aliens may have more consideration for contactees than humanity does.

Another, more likely, reason for abduction is that some of the intervention procedures require sophisticated medical and technical support. Because some (but not all) contact experiences appear to require removal to a controlled location, it's likely that at least some of the medical procedures involved are complex, delicate, and very difficult, if not dangerous. Remember, these are beings that possess the scientific knowledge to travel through interstellar space, pass through solid walls, and screen contactees' memories at will. If they find it necessary to remove contactees to a controlled location to ensure their safety, the medical procedures involved must be extraordinarily complex.

Why Take People at Night?

Although contact can occur during daylight hours, most people are taken at night, for the simple reason that it's easier. If you're going to remove individuals from their environment, it makes sense to do it at night, when they're least likely to be missed. (If I were to vanish in the middle of a meeting, there might be a few questions . . . although I must confess that I've attended a few meetings when an abduction probably would have been a blessing.)

It appears that the aliens are familiar with our daily activities and typical living patterns, and work within them. Since contact is occurring on a broad scale, it's not unreasonable to think that there may be a schedule involved, much like a follow-up appointment roster at a doctor's office, under which the aliens have a certain time window to pick up a contactee and do whatever has to be done. The logistics are likely staggering. It seems clear that the best solution for keeping on schedule without attracting undue attention to the process is to make the contacts at night. Unfortunately, some people seize on this nighttime aspect of the experience to assert that the contactee was merely dreaming and was not really abducted. This is incorrect. Psychologically healthy people are fully capable of knowing, after the fact, when they were dreaming and when they were awake.

Who Is Chosen?

It's not clear how individual contactees are chosen, or how many people have had contact or will have contact in the future. Attempts to find a common denominator among abductees has been unsuccessful so far. The choice doesn't appear to depend on social, political, or class distinctions. Dr. John Mack specifically commented on the diversity of his subjects. The contactees he worked with came from all walks of life and included a restaurant owner, secretaries, a prison guard, college students, a politician, and several housewives. Mack found no way to tie the nonabduction characteristics of these individuals' lives to their abduction stories, nor did he find a convincing psychodynamic link between the reported abduction experiences and other aspects of the abductees' personal histories or emotional lives.

It's worthwhile to stress once again that the contactees who have decided to seek professional help are psychologically normal people. In a blind study carried out for Budd Hopkins by psychologist Elizabeth Slater, nine abductees were given a standard battery of personality tests. The subjects proved to be nonpsychotic, but tended to suffer from anxiety and hypervigilance. In some cases, their self-concept appeared to be damaged, particularly in relation to sex. The study protocols and Dr. Slater's interpretations were checked by a second psychologist who agreed with the doctor's assessment. When Dr. Slater was subsequently told of the subjects' abduction claims, she considered their symptomatology to match the pattern that might be expected if such events had in fact taken place.

So we really have no clue as to how people are being chosen. Many contactees report that in addition to the physical examinations, they have been subjected to some form of psychological testing, or to other attempts to understand them and even bond with them. Some contactees report powerful "testing" experiences that suggest a continued psychological evaluation is taking place. Since most of our available scientific psychological data on this subject comes from people who have chosen to seek therapy or participate in psychological research, we are drawing conclusions based on a very select sample of contactees. Our conclusions thus will not be based on a truly representative sample of all human alien contact. What about those people who have found a balance with these beings and have no need to seek professional counselling? What about those who could not afford counselling if they thought they needed it? What about other cultures and countries in the world?

I believe that the aliens are focusing on people whom they consider to be compatible for the development of this new and very difficult relationship. This is not tough to understand; after all, in human relationships, what do we look for? Compatibility! We look for common values, a shared outlook, or other specific qualities that we think will help us in that specific relationship. The specific traits that the aliens are looking for is unclear. Although a study of contactees' psychological profiles may eventually shed some light on the psychological and spiritual qualities being sought, we simply don't have the tools or perspectives to assess people in the intimate way that the aliens appear to be able to.

We must be sure not to confer any kind of special status on contactees. Instead of arguing that contactees were chosen for high compatibility or because of their "visionary" qualities and ability to lead others, we could just as easily argue that they were picked earlier because they are the psychologically "slowest" students, and will need more help, or need it sooner, in order to assimilate their contact experiences. (I often suspect that the reason the aliens first unveiled themselves to me over twenty years ago is that I would need twenty years to come to grips with their presence!)

How Many People Are Affected?

In 1991, the Roper Organization conducted a survey that was aimed at estimating the number of people who might be involved in the abduction phenomenon. The sample of 5,947 adults, which was considered to represent 185,000,000 Americans, excluded anyone under the age of eighteen; all residents of Alaska and Hawaii; and those residing in group facilities such as dormitories, hospitals, etc. The chosen sample size was associated with a margin of error of ±1.4%. Survey results were as follows:

EVENT: Do You Remember . . . ?	Percentage Answering "Yes"*	Number of Americans Represented**
Waking up paralyzed with a sense of a strange person or presence or something else in the room.	18%	33,300,000
Experiencing a period of time of an hour or more in which you were apparently lost, but you could not remember why, or where you had been.	13%	24,050,000
Feeling that you were actually flying through the air although you didn't know why or how.	10%	18,500,000
Finding puzzling scars on your body and neither you nor anyone else remembering how you received them or where you got them.	8%	14,800,000
Seeing unusual lights or balls of light in a room without knowing what was causing them or where they came from.	8%	14,800,000

* margin of error: ± 1.4%

** In scaling up the study results, they were considered to represent a total of 185,000,000 Americans, even though that figure is actually smaller than the total US population. For example, when 8% of respondents reported that they had "seen unusual lights or balls of light in a room without knowing what was causing them or where they come from," the 8% of affirmative responses was said to represent a total of 14,800,000 Americans (.08 X 185,000,000).

Taken in isolation, each of these experiences can have other explanations. However, when a respondent answers "yes" to at least four of the five questions, there is a strong possibility that the individual is an abductee. The total number of respondents who answered "yes" to either four or five of the questions was 2% of the sample, or 199 people. Two percent of the 185,000,000 adult Americans represented by the Roper sample is just over 3,700,000 people. (As already pointed out, this figure excludes all children, the populations of Hawaii and Alaska, and anyone living in shared institutional quarters.)

Although it's difficult to react with equanimity to the fact that so many normal human beings are reporting these clusters of anomalous experiences, it's also important to point out that any attempt to quantify the numbers of people having contact is filled with logistical and scientific uncertainties. We still lack a definitive way to measure who has had contact and who has not. It's currently a very subjective activity. We can only be certain of one thing: the enormity of the contact has likely been underestimated.

In my description of the Winnipeg abduction experience, I purposefully omitted one important detail: while moving through the alien ship, I was escorted into a gymnasium-sized room that contained an estimated seventy beds. Although most of the beds were empty, about twenty or so were occupied by other people. They were of different ages and everyone was fully clothed in everyday wear, most with pants, shirts, and jackets, and some with nightgowns; one person with a red flannel shirt. There were no blankets on the beds. There was no movement or sounds coming from any of the people on the beds. They seemed to be in some sort of induced sleep. I don't know how I would have reacted had one just sat up or cried to me for help. It was damn upsetting. I thought, "Good God! What the hell is this?

I don't want to see this!" One might have thought that seeing another human being would have been a comforting sight. It certainly wasn't in my case.

In some ways, this momentary glimpse of large-scale contact, and the human helplessness it implied, was the most disturbing aspect of the entire experience. It was one thing to know it was happening to me, but quite another to know it was happening to so many other people on such a scale. There was no comfort in the sight of familiar human forms. Instead, the episode simply emphasized my complete lack of understanding and vulnerability in this situation.

Why Do People Report Different Kinds of Experiences?

People report different kinds of experiences for two basic reasons. First, the individual consciousness of each abductee is intimately involved, and second, the overall phenomenon is likely changing over time.

I believe that the aliens are trying not to frighten us unnecessarily, and as a result, they are constantly evaluating the psyche of each individual abductee to find the methods that produce effective results with minimal trauma. As a result, there will be differences in individual experiences. For example, I was allowed to perceive the aliens as having blue eyes with pupils, not the solid black eyes that many others have reported, because the aliens felt that this would help to reduce my fear. It also appears that they chose the car as the setting for my first abduction experience because it allowed me to still feel somewhat safe in my home as I worked on assimilating the first conscious contact experience. Other people may have their first abduction experience at home;

the flow of events likely depends at least in part on the psychology of the individual. The aliens spend a great deal of time and care on understanding individual contactees and trying to connect on an individual level. It therefore makes perfect sense that individual experiences will be different.

It also makes sense that the overall phenomenon is evolving over time. These beings come from a vastly different environment from ours, and it would be highly unreasonable to expect that there was no learning curve involved in their actions. Even within the human race, interaction between different societies often results in cultural faux pas. The cultural gap between humans and the aliens is many, many times wider than any gap between human cultures. Why should we expect that the aliens, no matter how benevolent their motives, are capable of understanding us perfectly?

The aliens have a goal for being here: they want something to change. The basic scientific methodology for changing any existing state of affairs is this: identify the problem, observe and understand the problem and the factors relevant to it, formulate ideas on how to improve the situation, introduce controlled changes, measure the results, and adjust your actions based on the results. If this is the basic paradigm that the aliens are following, it makes perfect sense that as they see our responses to their actions, they will adjust those actions for maximum effectiveness. Hence, as the aliens learn more about us (both as individuals and as a group), the overall pattern of the phenomenon will change over time.

What Can We Infer about the Aliens?

On a physical level, their species has to be highly adaptive to different environments. Most TV programs depict entering an alien world as a fairly simple thing to do. In reality, the process is fraught with difficulties. Consider just some of the possible variations between their world and ours: the strength of the gravitational field, composition of the atmosphere, ranges of temperature and humidity, and millions of different types of bacteria and viruses. The likelihood that their environment is identical to ours in all, or even most, of these respects is extremely low. The potential consequences to the aliens of a variation in any one of these factors could range from simple discomfort to death. Therefore, in order to work with us physically, they've had to make some significant physical adaptations. Their success in operating without space suits and interacting directly with a variety of human cultures suggests that they're an extraordinarily highly adaptable species. Just how they are able to achieve such adaptations may forever be a mystery.

As well as adapting to basic Earth conditions, the aliens must also cope with the potential problems of cross-cultural contamination. Throughout Earth's own history, the transmission of viruses and bacteria across sociocultural lines has caused catastrophic epidemics. Complete ecosystems have collapsed after the inadvertent introduction of a species not native to the system. It's not uncommon for anthropologists to interact with isolated tribes then, on returning some years later, find that the tribe is in serious trouble because the anthropologist has introduced foreign elements—be they infectious diseases or a taste for Coca-Cola—that the tribe is unable to cope with. (Within this context, the "decontamination" procedure I appear to have been put through on the ship makes perfect sense.)

The aliens appear to be highly organized and sophisticated with the ablity to carefully plan and implement complex actions. For example, in Winnipeg, they were able to locate me when I was over 1,300 km from my home. It seems reasonable to assume they carefully assessed the local environment where I parked my car. They decided to use some form of mental suggestion on a truck driver so he would park his rig to block my car from view of the people in the diner, and they orchestrated the act of returning me and the car in a similar way.

The construction of their ship also showed a high degree of organization and planning. As I moved through the ship with the small beings, it became obvious that the proportions of the architecture were all geared towards beings of *human* size. The implications of this observation were staggering. They built this huge craft specifically to deal with human beings.

Another interesting characteristic of the aliens is that they may have the ability to bend the laws of time and space. Sometimes they appear to exist in an environment where both time and space work differently from how they do on Earth. One night when they entered my room, I observed their movements briefly while in full waking consciousness. They appeared to be ghostly images or shadows: I could see right through them! In spite of this, they were interacting with the physical surroundings just like solid beings would. I could hear the thumping of feet and the sounds of furniture being moved. Their own physical movements were extremely odd; they appeared to be moving far too fast, as if I were watching a movie in super-fast forward. I wondered if my visual perceptions were being altered, but since sounds seemed to be normal in pitch, it seemed unlikely. I do know that their movements were definitely not consistent with the space and time dimensions that I'm familiar with.

They are beings quite unlike us, struggling to operate within our world and perhaps doing it imperfectly. The results can be unnerving, exhilarating, disquieting, and sometimes terrifying. Curiously enough, many abductees have reported that, at times, the aliens seem to be afraid of us! I have little doubt they have suffered emotionally, or even physically, from some encounters with humans. They have good reason to be cautious around us. It's been over twenty years, and I still don't know much more about them. I don't even know their names. I don't know their plans, or where they come from, or when my next contact is going to be. I can only hope that, over time, our relationship will become more open.

Socially and culturally, I expect that the aliens are very different from us. Their social structure seems, in some ways, to resemble that of a bee colony—there seem to be different roles within their social structure, and within those roles, they appear to manifest a "collective mind." During my contacts, it occasionally seemed that they had trainees along—new members of their species that they were educating in the process of interacting with humans.

I observed a real sense of oneness among them, recognition of duties and a sense that they work within a common purpose. At the same time, there is also a palpable sense of individuality. When the being gave me her name during the meditation contact, there was a strong sense of a unique and individual presence. The fact that she had an individual name is worth noting.

Perhaps this is their special gift, to be able to combine their sense of individuality with a shared intimacy among individuals that has no equivalent here on Earth. When I was given the original message during meditation, the three simultaneous messages ("We're here to help you, and we're here to help your friends, and we're here to help all of humanity") were combined and contained in a single thought that viewed human beings as far less separate than we are used to seeing ourselves. It may be that the goal of this entire intervention is to help us make this shift in perspective. After all, it's much more difficult to harm those we feel truly connected to.

Whatever the aliens' social structure, it's like nothing we've ever had in human history. Perhaps that's where this intervention is taking us—to a new kind of social structure. That is something we'll have to decide for ourselves. However, one thing is clear: when we analyze the aliens' actions, a picture emerges of one or more kinds of beings who have made incalculable sacrifices and taken risks just to interact with us. Hardly the cold, clinical aliens of lore.

What sort of reality does a consciousness more advanced than ours inhabit? I don't know. One thing I do know is that their reality is in some way deeper than ours. In their presence I feel, not humbled, exactly, but as if I'm in kindergarten. It's as if I'm standing around with a bunch of teachers, and they just know so much *more* than I do. It's not just a simple question of knowledge. It's a matter of enlightenment, and the integration of knowledge and spirituality at a very deep level.

Do They Care about Us?

I believe they care deeply. The aliens are very aware of who we are as individuals, and I believe that within the requirements of the intervention, they're trying to make the contact experience as easy for us as possible. They're very careful about selecting what I call the *initiating event*—the first conscious contact—during which they let you know that they exist and that they are involved in your life.

The recall patterns of contactees tend to support the idea that the aliens prefer to break the news of their involvement in a human life gradually. It's not uncommon for people who've had conscious contact to look back over their lives and realize that the aliens had been present for some time before the contactee became aware of it. This is likely done to make things easier for the contactee. I, for one, found great reassurance in the idea that even though contact had likely been going on for some time, I was still alive, healthy, and whole.

In my case, it was the paralysis that I felt during the first abduction encounter that provided an important clue. It was absolutely identical to the paralysis that I'd felt on various occasions throughout my life. Every four years or so, I would wake up in bed feeling as if I were paralyzed and unable to move. (These experiences date back to the early 1960s, well before I ever encountered the idea that paralysis was a common occurrence during abduction.) By allowing me to feel and remember these paralysis events, the aliens were planting seeds of knowledge for me to interpret later. As a result, at the time of the abduction I was able to think back and realize that contact had already been occurring over much of my life. (I have some disdain for the theory of sleep paralysis that has been proposed by researchers to explain away the phenomenon. To me, the idea that sleep paralysis is some sort of aberration of the brain's sleep/wake cycle just doesn't hold up.)

Unquestionably, it's a shock to realize that there's a whole part of your life that you had no idea existed. In some respects, it's like waking up from a coma and gradually piecing together the past elements of your life. For example, I now know that at some time before the Winnipeg encounter, an implant was placed behind my right ear, and this implant was used during the Winnipeg encounter to administer treatment. Yet I had no knowledge of the implant until long after it was put in place.

So, yes, the aliens do care about us. In situations where they cause human beings discomfort or fear, I know they are aware of our reactions. They're cognizant of our fears and they try not to frighten us unnecessarily, but our fears will not deter them from doing what they're here to do. They carry out their unfathomable (to us) tasks with a sense of purpose and direction. Their actions exude a belief in the "rightness" of their actions—almost as if there has been a calling, or perhaps a call to arms. In compensation for the difficult aspects of the experiences, they do try to support contactees by communicating deep feelings of love and compassion. During one encounter, just as I was being removed from my bed, one of the small beings kissed my right arm. It was an impulsive kiss, filled with love and kindness. Why would a kiss mean so much to this being (a member of a species that was so physically different from me)? Obviously, there was a deepening relationship unfolding.

They don't want to scare us or hurt us, but as our world moves closer to nuclear and environmental disaster, time is running short. As the situation worsens, they have less and less opportunity to influence positive change in a slow, controlled way. For this reason alone, the phenomenon is likely to become much more intense in the near future.

The aliens aren't gods. They're not perfect. No matter how benevolent their intentions, they can't make this intervention easy for us. I am in no way discounting the pain, terror, and upheaval that contactees feel, but it's a fact that every human endeavour that has the power to make people happy—love, marriage, sex, work, parenthood—also has the power to cause pain. This intervention is about saving the human race and the other living things on the planet. If there are individual sacrifices to be made, we will need the courage to accept that fact and reach out despite our fears.

It's important to note that although the aliens are more evolved than humans, they don't perceive us as being inferior. They don't think in those terms. They see us as a different expression of life, one that is out of balance and, as a consequence, in danger. They truly want to connect with us and help us past that. Parenthood can be used as an appropriate metaphor: a good parent, although more evolved than the child, does not look down on the child, but helps and teaches it. Parents want the best for their children, but sometimes tough love is necessary. The aliens don't see themselves as superior, and neither should we view them in that way. Is the parent superior to the child? Many parents say that their children teach them! What's involved here is a difference of perspective. Instead of thinking of the aliens as smarter, we should be trying to define what might be involved for the human race to move to a higher level of consciousness.

Let's Think about Them for a Moment . . .

If we weren't so busy thinking about ourselves, we'd realize that the contact process is probably not easy on the aliens either. They certainly don't enjoy scaring the bejesus out of millions of people. They don't enjoy administering painful medical procedures or dealing with screaming angry violent human beings.

What is the real relationship between us, then? Years ago, when I'd just undergone some of the worst shocks of the encounter process and was desperately praying for understanding, the answer came in a most unusual way.

I was at a party, trying to take some comfort in the presence of others, when a very large, very boisterous, very drunk Vietnam vet started scaring the heck out of everyone. He wasn't angry or abusive—far from it. He was so far "up" he was almost manic—but he was so drunkenly unrestrained in his happiness that his behavior was frightening everyone. Although I was a bit nervous about it too, I was somehow drawn to the man. I introduced myself, thinking I might try to calm him down. After we'd talked for a while, the vet explained that the reason he was so happy was that he was celebrating great news: a boy he was caring for had successfully fought off a deadly type of cancer.

It was a fascinating story. As a volunteer Big Brother, the veteran had been paired with a teenager of almost eighteen years who, because of a mental impairment, had the mental capacity of a four-year-old. The boy, who felt completely healthy, had been diagnosed with cancer, and his single mother had consented to a long-term program of difficult and painful chemotherapy treatments.

During the course of the treatments, the boy began to see the hospital as a place that hurt him and made him feel sick. He didn't have the mental capacity to understand why he was going there. He felt fine—except when his mother took him to the hospital. Before long, he began to suspect that his mother was trying to hurt him and became physically violent whenever she tried to put him into the car to go for treatment.

That was the point at which the veteran had been assigned to the family to help manage the boy. "Oh, man," he confided to me, "her son, he really started to hate her. Sometimes he wouldn't talk to her for days. I've seen a lot in my life, but I've never seen anyone as strong as that woman. She loved him so much that she was willing to do whatever it took to save him. Even if it meant he might hate her for the rest of her life."

His eyes filled with tears as he told me about a day when the woman stood nearby and watched him muscle the boy into the car. Her son gave her the most scornful, hate-filled glare that the veteran had ever seen. "Jim," he told me, "that woman stood there with tears running down her face—not for herself, but for her son. That is the greatest love I've ever seen from anybody."

Listening to him talk, I was flooded with sadness, even a touch of shame. The story was an obvious parallel to my experiences with the aliens. *I was that boy.* Here I was, feeling healthy and thinking everything was fine, but in fact, both humanity and I were suffering from a terminal illness we don't understand and that requires a medical intervention. The aliens were in my life because of some threat that I did not have the capacity to fully understand, and quite possibly never would. For the first time, I started to think how difficult it must be for them. They were just like that mother. How could I have been so selfish that I did not even consider that the actions they were taking might be painful and difficult for them too?

Humanity may never know all the aliens' motives. It's possible, albeit highly unlikely, that their survival somehow depends on ours. It's also possible that they are doing this for purely altruistic, spiritually oriented reasons. Whatever their motives, some things are already clear: they're not here for our technology; their technology is vastly superior to ours. They're not here for our resources; they don't think in terms of taking things away from others. I believe that the aliens are here helping us because humanity has something to offer the universe. Maybe not right away, and maybe not for a long time, but I do think that somehow we must have an important role to play in the overall evolution of the universe. Maybe they are simply helping us past this rough spot in our development so that we can become all we were meant to be.

How Much Time Do We Have?

"I know not with what weapons World War III will be fought, but World War IV will be fought with sticks and stones."
—Albert Einstein

During abductions, contactees are often shown images of planet-wide devastation. The question becomes: if these images are intended to give us a visceral understanding of the dangers we are facing, how much time do we have to prevent such events from happening?

As far as the notion of time goes, I've already noted that the aliens appear to have the ability to alter some space/time characteristics. However, humanity lives in the space/time environment found on Earth, so unless our conscious perspectives change, this is the system we need to work within. If the event of concern is nuclear war, current political tensions and global conflicts suggest that the next twenty- to thirty-year period will be critical. Similarly, if the triggering event is ecological catastrophe, the next twenty to thirty years will be critical, because we're fast approaching the point where we'll be unable to reverse the damage that we are inflicting on our environment.

Another way to estimate the time frame may be to look at the ages of the earlier contactees. Although it's generally accepted that the UFO phenomenon began to manifest in its present form in the mid-1940s, the abductions did not start at that time, but approximately fifteen years later, around 1955. Given that the aliens seem to be modifying the nervous systems of individual contactees, as discussed in detail later in this book, it's reasonable to assume that they are expecting some change or "payoff" within the lifetimes of these individuals. In other words, the time scale for the intervention must be linked to the general life expectancies of the contactees who are experiencing medical procedures that induce some sort of change.

Any calculations in this vein are estimates that involve a large number of uncertainties. Assuming the aliens' medical activities will not extend the average life expectancy, then it's useful to speculate on when something might happen. In the 1940s, the average life expectancy in the Western world was about 65 years of age. By the 1990s, it had reached 75 years of age. Of the forty-one abductees that Dr. John Mack worked with prior to the end of 1992, the oldest was 57 years of age. Assuming a seventy-five-year life expectancy, that person could expect to live another eighteen years. This would give us a minimum time reference of around 2010. Given that this example uses the age of the oldest contactee, we can assume that the critical period is likely somewhere between 2010 and 2020. Incidentally, the year 2012 marks the completion of the major Mayan cycle of the Long Count that began in 3114 BCE. In 2012, the Mayan calendar "turns over" to begin a new era. One wonders if the ancients have some glimpse of what is coming.

All indications are that time is short. This is why I believe that UFO sightings will continue to increase in frequency, and that we'll see the craft more often over more heavily populated areas. The number of people recalling encounter or abduction experiences will also increase in the coming years. In my opinion, it's likely that a much larger proportion of the human race, if not all of us, will be aware of the aliens' existence by 2010 to 2020. We have very little time to prepare.

4

WHAT'S HAPPENING?

"It is of the highest importance in the art of detection to be able to recognize, out of a number of facts, which are incidental and which vital. Otherwise your energy and attention must be dissipated instead of being concentrated."
—Sherlock Holmes

The abduction experience involves a variety of medical procedures and psychological interactions. Not all contactees report being involved in the same activities. Reviewing the reports for commonalities does, however, suggest certain patterns of actions on the part of the aliens. Analyzing these patterns can help us develop a hypothesis and predictions about the intervention process.

Some Ruminations on Memory

Much of the information in this book is derived from a combination of abductees' conscious recollections and memories retrieved via hypnotic regression. For that reason, it's appropriate to make some observations on the nature of memory.

Are the Memories Real?

Memories can be slippery things. We may remember that we had fish for dinner last week—but was it on Tuesday or Wednesday? We may remember that it was Tuesday—but will we remember that a week from now? A month from now? If someone swears that we went to a particular movie with them two years ago, will we remember the plot? Conversely, if we remember the plot of a movie we saw four years ago, is it because we really saw that movie, or because four years ago we had an intense daydream, during which we speculated about the movie and cooked up a probable plot?

Ask any criminal lawyer if eyewitness testimony is foolproof, and you will be told that it is not. One witness swears the car was blue. To another it was green. If the car is found, it may well turn out to be red.

However much the above arguments may appear to cast doubts on the reliability of memories, they have one characteristic in common: they apply to events that are *otherwise unremarkable.* If a person has no particular reason to remember, the boundaries of memory can be fuzzy indeed. Traumatic and highly important situations are another matter. When a person is *aware in the moment* that an unusual or important event is taking place, the event tends to be burned into memory. In the most traumatic cases, people often cannot forget things they would rather not remember.

Some therapists have attempted to explain abduction accounts as "screen memories" that mask repressed sexual abuse. In a screen memory, the mind somehow fabricates a "memory" of an event that did not really happen, in order to mask the memory of an event that did happen. However, psychologists familiar with the phenomenon state that no abduction memories have ever been stripped away to reveal a past history of sexual abuse.

By contrast, screen memories have frequently been stripped away to reveal a history of abduction. For example, memories of seeing owls with abnormally large eyes are often screen memories masking an abduction encounter.

It's important to remember that most contact encounters take place in an altered state of consciousness, and we are not certain how this affects recall. My own contact memories vary in focus. Some are absolutely clear, as fully lucid as every other important waking memory. These contact episodes are easy to recall at any time, simply because of their intensity and clarity. Other memories concern events that took place in a state between dreaming and waking. It could be that they're real, but there's always an element of doubt. Thirdly, there is a category of experiences that may well be dream states: these are events that I consider not real, but perhaps are my subconscious's way of dealing with other events that are real.

Categorizing my contact-related memories into the above three categories has been useful. I know what I can count on to be true, what might be true, and what may be metaphorically true, but is perhaps not real. Other abductees report the same ability to differentiate between events that might have happened and events that *did* happen.

Is Hypnotic Regression the Answer?

It appears that during some contact episodes, the aliens induce a powerful alternate state of consciousness in the contactee, in order to safely manage the interaction. (During one of my encounters, it felt like a tight band of energy was squeezing my head, and I could feel myself drifting towards a state of consciousness that resembled deep meditation.) As a result, many memories of abduction encounters are acquired during this altered state of consciousness, giving the memories a disjointed or dreamlike quality. In other cases, the contactee simply perceives that there is a block of "missing time," during which he or she has no memories at all.

Some contactees have turned to hypnosis to help them remember their experiences. Because the memories have been acquired, and suppressed, at another level of consciousness, it should be no surprise that inducing an altered state of consciousness is an effective way to help recall them. (It should, however, be noted that there is no guarantee that all repressed memories can be recalled via hypnosis.)

Many contactees, including me, have discovered that at the end of each episode the aliens instructed us not to remember and shifted our consciousness so that we could not remember the bulk of the experience. The non-ordinary state of consciousness induced via hypnosis appears to help lift this prohibition, so that the abductee can more easily retrieve memories that were blocked from normal consciousness.

One drawback to hypnotic regression is that it can, if poorly handled, produce distorted or false memories. For this reason, it's useful to know how many contactees' memories were obtained via hypnosis and how many come from fully conscious recall. A PEER survey found that just under half the abductees had never been hypnotized, so their accounts could not be attributed to hypnotic distortion. Even more telling was the study's discovery that 97% of the abductees who chose to undergo hypnosis did so *because* they had preexisting conscious memories of the abduction and chose to use hypnosis to investigate those existing memories more fully.

Nonetheless, we must be cautious about relying on hypnosis. It will always be possible for an informed person to mislead an investigator, or for a well-meaning but inexperienced investigator to lead the contactee into producing false information. However, it bears repeating that Dr. John Mack did not find contactees to be fantasy-prone individuals, but healthy people who were accurately reporting their experiences.

How Can Memories Be Suppressed?

Unless a person has actually experienced the memory-alteration phenomenon, it seems incredible that entire blocks of memory can be replaced with screen memories or simply blanked out. One of my own experiences will illustrate the strength of the phenomenon.

As mentioned earlier, I had puzzled over the differences between the way Whitley Strieber described the aliens' eyes (solid black and insect-like) and my own observations (blue pupils and a human eye structure), and had concluded that they were the same beings, but I was perceiving them differently. One evening, some time after I'd come to this conclusion, the aliens came into my bedroom, floated me out of bed (right through the covers), and I found myself in a sitting position.

I didn't want to open my eyes. Although I knew by then that they were rather shy and could get uncomfortable if you looked at them, that wasn't the main reason. As with the initial contact experience, I was afraid that if I actually looked at them I might lose control, and I didn't want to do that. I wanted these contacts to continue. So, not wanting to damage the emerging relationship, I was trying to suppress my sensory system so I could stay calm enough to communicate. I wanted them to know that in spite of my fears, I was starting to understand the relationship and I truly wanted to communicate with them. Feeling regrets about my past behavior, I barely managed to utter the words through my paralysis, "I'm sorry."

In the middle of removing me from the room, they stopped. The paralysis subsided and the being beside me said, "Whaaaaaattt?" The voice had a very lyrical quality, with an intense note of curiosity. "I'm sorry," I repeated more clearly. There was silence. No movement, no sound. It seemed as if they were waiting for me to do something. I said, "I can't open my eyes because I might be afraid of the way you look."

The alien said, "I'll have to remember that."

It was an unexpected response. "I knew it," I blurted out triumphantly. "I knew you could change appearance!"

In a rather haughty and disdainful tone the alien immediately replied, "Oh. I knew we had a *bright* one here."

The response was so distant and detached that I immediately wanted to apologize. The comment had not been a compliment. It was clear that in their eyes I had elevated myself above other people by saying that I knew something that other people didn't. My immediate reaction was, "Whoa, whoa. Hold it. I didn't mean it to be insulting." Then I realized that they were trying to tell me that even though I may know a bit more than another person does, it doesn't mean that I can put myself above that person. More knowledge does not correlate to being a better person, or entitle me to elevate myself above someone else. It's as if they had said, "Jim, you have a tendency to elevate yourself above other people by thinking that way, and when you do, it separates you from others, and that is not good."

I really thought about that afterwards. It was a valuable lesson. I believe they were showing me how I should consider dealing with people who openly attack me for my statements and opinions.

The interesting point about this story is that when I think back on the episode, I can remember everything about it clearly, except for one word in one sentence that the alien spoke. The sentence is, "Oh. I knew we had a *bright* one here," and the word that is missing is "bright." Because I do remember the meaning of the sentence and the events around it, I can infer that the word is "bright," but in my auditory recall of the event, I cannot hear that one word in focus. It's a dramatic difference. The rest of it, I can hear perfectly. "Oh. I knew we had a . . . one here." It's clarity, clarity, fuzzy, clarity, clarity. I have no doubt that they did this as a sort of object lesson. The degree of power that's required to be able to blank out one word in an otherwise clear recollection is amazing.

Why Should We Remember Anything?

Because the memory screens can be so powerful, perhaps the key question isn't "how do they make abductees forget about their experiences?" but *why are abductees allowed to remember anything about their experiences?* This is a crucial point, one missed by many researchers. Some people in the field of UFO investigation have become so preoccupied with uncovering what people don't remember that they've overlooked the golden chalice of understanding: what *do* people remember?

The assumption is that the conscious memories are nothing but accidental snippets of information that didn't get properly suppressed, while the really important information has been blocked out. In fact, the opposite is true. If the aliens have the full ability (and they do) to block out all memories, then why should abductees remember anything?

The obvious answer is that the aliens want them to remember. The memories are specifically selected and permitted for just that reason. As described earlier, there appears to be an overall strategy that involves multiple stages of exposure, with particular care taken to addressing the psychological health of the individual. The memories that are allowed to surface are very carefully chosen. Many contactees have reported a gradual unfolding of memory, during which they slowly reclaimed the knowledge of a series of experiences stretching back through their lives.

Until a person has experienced it, it's hard to appreciate how fully a person can be prevented from recalling early experiences until the "right time." How can one forget something for so many years, then suddenly remember it with full clarity? How can certain episodes simply be blanked from your waking consciousness? I don't know. I simply know it can be done, and that very few elements of a contactee's experience are left to chance. This is why I believe that our studies should concentrate on contactees' conscious memories, because they contain the information that the interaction was intended to deliver to the contactee's conscious mind.

After undergoing hypnotic regression, I realized that the additional memories did not dramatically improve my understanding of the phenomenon nor deepen my relationship with the aliens. I came to understand that all my conscious memories of the experience—every last detail—had been selected for a specific purpose. Each conscious memory had a reason. The aliens wanted me to know that they had been involved in my life for a very long time, and that they will continue to be involved in my life even though I may not have conscious recollections of some contacts. They wanted me to know that if I chose to try to remember, the process could be painful and frightening. They also wanted me to know that they were conducting some type of biomedical intervention that involved attempts to change something within my central nervous system (CNS). The significance of these memories cannot be overstated. Ultimately, the insights that I gained from the conscious memories of the encounters were all that I really needed to know.

By comparing the conscious memories of a large number of abductees, it's clear that the aliens *want* contactees to know that some form of physical intervention is taking place.

For example, since a large number of abductees have conscious memories involving medical procedures, we should assume that these procedures will be of some importance to the future relationship. As described in the next section, some of my own strongest memories involve the physical aspects of contact. I believe that the aliens want us to understand that this physical aspect is a major, if not critical, component of the intervention and our emerging relationship with them.

If my observations about the workings of contactees' memories are valid, then it's possible the memory screens are intended to function as protection—a sort of psychological Band-Aid for the developing consciousness. If so, undertaking hypnosis too soon could be a grave mistake. In a society that seeks knowledge at almost any cost, such a perspective might seem strange. However, I believe that one purpose of the screens is to prevent the abductee from recalling experiences so fresh and frightening that their immediate recall would endanger the person's ability to remain sane and productive. Even though I recall some encounters, I know, from a variety of physical aftereffects, that I've had many encounters that never entered my waking consciousness. If I were to remember every detail of every one of these experiences, it would certainly create some strong psychological and emotional challenges!

"Go slowly and carefully" seems to be the order of the day. The benefits of conducting hypnosis should be considered carefully, and each case evaluated on an individual basis. Hypnosis should certainly never be made a routine (much less compulsory!) practice for everyone who has had a contact experience. It's also important to remember that people in many other cultures do not have access to hypnotherapy. It may be useful to investigate how these other cultures interpret the phenomenon, and what therapies, if any, they use.

Medical Interventions

Many abductees report undergoing a variety of medical procedures. Some of these procedures seem to be purely investigative, while others appear intended to change the abductee's physical status in some way. The purpose of the investigative procedures is relatively easy to infer: for some reason, the aliens need to understand how our bodies work. The procedures that change the abductee's physical status are harder to draw inferences from.

There is evidence that the contact process involves some kind of biophysical modification centered on the human central nervous system. The purpose of this modification is not yet known with certainty. There are three basic possibilities. Perhaps the aliens are changing our bodies to facilitate communication between our species. Perhaps they are making physical changes that will stimulate the evolution of human consciousness, so that we interact differently with the world around us. Or perhaps they are changing our bodies because such changes will be necessary for us to survive whatever is coming. Or perhaps there is another possibility that we haven't yet considered.

Implants

I must confess this is one area that I hesitated writing about at length. It is just so darn bizarre. I do know that telling someone that an alien put something in my brain is pretty crazy. For heaven's sake, I would run not walk away from someone who introduced me to such an idea. I would probably worry more about someone who automatically believed such an outrageous claim. So why say anything? The only rationale is that these beings wanted me know that implants do exist and therefore I should mention it.

It's common for abductees to report that the aliens have implanted one or more devices or objects in the contactee's body for some unknown purpose. So it's reasonable to assume that since these beings are conducting a widespread intervention that involves the physical human body, the implants will have a specific function or functions. We should look for implants that are found in the same place in many abductees, and/or function the same way within a variety of human carriers. Finding and studying these implants could yield important clues.

To my knowledge, no one has yet recovered any object from a contactee's body that has proved, without doubt, to be an implant. There are many reasons that this proof hasn't yet been obtained. No full-scale search has been made. We still don't know exactly what we're looking for. There may be more than one type of implant, with each type significantly different in location and design, depending on its purpose. Some abductees carrying implants will be unaware of their presence. And last, but not least, it's possible that since the aliens have made some effort to keep their activities secret, they may have deliberately constructed the implants to be difficult to detect. The issue of searching for implants is addressed in detail in chapter 8 on science. If nothing else, obtaining definitive evidence of implants would help us to prove the extraterrestrial presence and, more importantly, help us to evaluate who has had contact and who has not.

My own implant is located behind my right ear, in roughly the same horizontal plane as the ear canal and just under the skin. The only reminders of its presence are an occasional mild

soreness or irritation of the area, and a slight bump (not the mas-
toid bone) just under the skin—soft, spongy, and about the size
of a pencil eraser head. I've known about this bump since about
age nine, but never knew what it was until it was used by the
aliens in a way I'll describe shortly. As a result of that experience,
I now know that the implant is a thin, needle-like structure a few
inches long that passes through the skull into the deeper parts of
the brain before branching off. The outer end has a flat receptor
head of less than ¼ inch in diameter. Its location, directly behind
the ear, is ideal for a subcutaneous receptor designed to conduct
electrical current to the brain, since the area doesn't have much
hair. I don't know what the implant is constructed of, but it's
probably very similar in structure to a nerve. It has to be flexible,
to accommodate the movement of the head and neck, and allow
for a relatively good seal between the different layers of the brain
and skull. The implant is not visible on X-rays, which suggests only
that its density is similar to that of the surrounding tissue. It may
well be constructed of organic tissue that's genetically similar to my
own. For anyone who doesn't know it's there, it's very easy to miss.

One way to confirm the implant's presence might be to apply
a small electrical stimulus to it and measure the brain response.
However, it's not clear what kind of risk would be involved, nor
what the results of applying an inappropriate level of stimulation
might be.

I do know what happens when the implant is stimulated
by the aliens. The full story of this experience is a combination
of conscious memory and information gathered from hypnotic
regression. The occasion in question took place on the aliens' ship.
I had been taken into a room about two stories high that had an
elevated walkway with railings around its perimeter. In the room
were bright lights and a great deal of complex, computerized-
looking equipment. Although I have no definite recollection of

how many aliens were there, the area seemed very busy. I was placed on a table. Without warning, some kind of object penetrated my left side, pushing into my internal organs. I could feel it deep inside me but didn't know what it was doing. There was a sensation as if my stomach were filling up, and then the object was pulled out.

Next, a device came down by my right ear. One of the most unnerving parts of this experience was that this device seemed to possess its own consciousness. It was a multi-articulated arm that had no joints and moved like an octopus's arm. It was mechanical, yet it also seemed alive. It was completely unnerving. The device touched the right side of my head, just behind the ear, delivering an electrical shock.

The shock went straight into my brain, as if it were following a path along a wire. I felt it follow that specific path, then branch out like the roots on a plant. The shock stimulated a response that I now know is characteristic of electrically stimulating the brain: it induced convulsions. Along with the convulsions, I began vomiting up a pink solution—I had to assume it was the substance that had been injected into my stomach by the probe that penetrated my side. (In the hypnotic recall of the event, not only did I remember having convulsions, I started convulsing right on the spot and having dry heaves that mimicked the vomiting.)

I now know that the process I was subjected to is very similar to a process called electroconvulsive therapy (ECT) that is used in human medicine to affect the function of the brain and central nervous system. We know that consciousness is intimately linked to brain function, and that specific brain structures are responsible for controlling the endocrine system and the body's other internal environmental controls.

When using ECT to induce convulsions, human medicine uses a combination of anesthesia and muscle relaxants to ease the process. The aliens do not administer any form of anesthesia or muscle relaxants before initiating their procedures. It's possible that such nerve-suppressing chemicals might counteract the changes that the stimulation is intended to achieve. At any rate, the convulsions stimulated by the procedure are extremely uncomfortable. Like other abductees, I've experienced a great deal of muscle soreness after some of these encounters.

(By the way, I'm the wrong guy to ask about comparing scars. The probe that went into my side left no scar at all. In my experience, the aliens' technology allows for penetration of the body without leaving any kind of scar or mark. Whatever the answer, I still can't play "my-scar-is-bigger-than-your-scar," because I don't have any scars that I can't account for.)

It seems fairly clear that the aliens are trying to stimulate changes in the human nervous system. Given the time-sensitive nature of these contacts, implants make perfect sense. If you have to stimulate an area more than once, it makes sense to put a mechanism in place so you can do so with a minimum of effort. It's rather like leaving an IV needle in the arm of a hospital patient who'll need a lot of transfusions or intravenous injections. An abductee's implant need only be touched by a stimulating device to deliver the appropriate impulse to the correct area of the brain or body.

One night years ago, I woke up knowing immediately that something was terribly wrong with my body. I'd had illnesses and injuries before, but this was something completely different. I could feel patches of heat and cold all over my body. Parts of my skin felt red-hot, while others felt like ice. Far more frightening was the sense that my internal organs were shutting down. It was as if something had gone wrong with my central nervous system, and my body was systematically malfunctioning and shutting down. It was the strangest sensation I had ever felt; I could actually feel myself dying. It was not a dream. I was awake, experiencing full and normal consciousness, and my life was draining away. I thought about dialing 911, but I had no strength to even get out of bed. It wasn't a paralysis, I simply had no strength, not even to stagger out to my living room to the phone. I couldn't move. I simply lay there, knowing that it was the end and trying to prepare myself.

Then the aliens came into the room. It must have been only ten or fifteen seconds from the time I'd felt the first sensations, but it seemed like an eternity. One of the aliens concentrated on my head, while others went for my throat and chest area. That's all I consciously remember. I woke with a start the next morning, feeling fine. Clearly, they must have been monitoring my vital signs and had been prepared in case there was trouble. This leads me to believe that the event was an unfortunate by-product of some of their medical procedures. Whatever they're trying to do with human beings is pushing their technology, and our bodies, to their limits. It appears that they're learning as much as we're learning through this process, and that there are bumps and hurdles on the road. But the speed of their response was extraordinary and suggested a high degree of planning and preparation for such emergencies.

Given that the aliens' procedures seem to be targeting the human brain and central nervous system, it seems reasonable to start looking there for implants and physiological anomalies. I'm betting that other contactees will have an electricity-conducting device similar to mine located behind one ear. Because this kind of implant can be easily detected by external touch, it may be able to serve as a simple diagnostic tool for assessing and categorizing some individuals who report abduction experiences.

The question arises: should such implants be removed? My feeling is that since the implants are intended to improve the well-being of the abductee, their removal should not be encouraged. I suggest studying them under controlled conditions with non-intrusive techniques. Given that the implants seem designed to change the brain/CNS function, it may be reasonable to consider looking for structural and/or functional changes in the hypothalamus and pituitary areas of the brain.

Body as Microenvironment

The human body can be thought of as a microenvironment that has developed and evolved within the larger (macro) environment or the world around us. Each human being is a biological microenvironment living in some degree of harmony with its planetary surroundings. We have evolved over time to exist successfully within a specific macroenvironment that includes our planet's water, air, food, bacteria, viruses, and other living creatures.

If the aliens are changing something within our central nervous system, they are in effect altering the microenvironment of our bodies. The question is, why?

One possibility is that they know that the macroenvironment around us is going to change, and they are preparing us. Another possibility is that they're stimulating our spiritual development (microenvironment) so we are moved to interact differently with the macroenvironment that we have, in other words, with the Earth.

Some cultures postulate the existence of specific body energy systems like chakras, acupuncture meridian lines, and so on. It's quite possible that there are energy systems in our bodies that we don't yet understand, and the aliens are trying to stimulate the development of these systems to help us in the coming transition.

A variety of medical procedures may be used. One night I was lying on my stomach in bed, fully awake, when I began to feel that something was going to happen. Then the paralysis started. I heard a small noise, and there was a sense of presence beside me. I felt a pressure on the back of my head, as if something were being pushed through the skull into my brain. There was a sound like a crunching apple. No pain, just the crunching sound. I was totally lucid and awake, but unable to move. Suddenly I felt a liquid being injected into my brain. There was a bizarre, spreading sense of coolness as the liquid flowed over the folds of the outer layer (the cortex) of the brain. I could actually feel it flow over my brain. Suddenly, the object was pulled out, and the alien was gone. I promptly went to sleep. (This kind of calm reaction to such a strange experience may seem odd, but the aliens appear to have a way of commanding specific responses from contactees.)

The Role of Perception

"There are things known and there are things unknown,
and in between are the doors of perception."
—Aldous Huxley

One reason the aliens are trying to change our central nervous system may be that the CNS is intimately related to consciousness—and the role of consciousness in this contact process may be far greater than we think.

Is reality independent of consciousness? Humans have a set of senses, and we use these to perceive and interact with the world around us. What would our relationship be with beings who had a totally different set of senses? Would we be invisible to them, and they to us? Could we inhabit the same physical space, yet be completely unaware of one another? Might they help us to develop sensory systems more like theirs, so we could share their physical and mental perceptions?

Human senses operate via receptors. We have retinas, so we see. We have proprioceptors, so we feel touch. At the biochemical level, our body function is highly dependent on various receptors. What if our receptors malfunction or atrophy? Our body function changes. We go blind. We go deaf. Malfunctions occur at the cellular level as well. For example, in a physical condition called hyperinsulemia, the body's insulin receptors become desensitized to the hormone insulin. The insulin is present in the bloodstream, often in high concentrations, and ready to enter the cell, but the cell's receptors simply do not perceive it. As far as the cell is concerned, the insulin does not exist.

Do humans have residual sense receptors that we no longer use? It's common for small children to report interactions with invisible beings. In our culture, children are told that the beings are not real, and as a result, the sightings usually stop as the child ages. In other cultures, where the phenomenon is considered normal, it is more likely to persist into adulthood. In Mexico, for example, many adults report seeing spirits or otherworldly beings, and although the sightings themselves may be perceived as frightening, they are assumed to be true events that in no way indicate mental disturbance on the part of the perceiver.

The obvious question arises: do humans have sense receptors that have atrophied over time? More than that: do we have sense receptors that our species has never been able to fully develop? Can our nervous system be enhanced to receive stimuli that we currently cannot perceive? (I can't resist a computer-based analogy: if we get a new plug-in card, can we perform new functions?)

If the aliens' actions are aimed at changing our consciousness, they might be trying to help us see them or each other and/or enable us to have the direct "meeting of consciousness" that is so much a part of abduction experiences, and which has no parallel in human life. In my contact experiences, I have been able to directly perceive the aliens' thoughts and emotions. Are the implants helping give me this capacity for direct mental connection with them or other human beings? Time will tell.

Even if it's true that one purpose of the implants is to help us interact with the aliens, our seeing them must be not an end in itself, but only a means to an end. What is the ultimate goal? I think the ultimate goal of contact is to stimulate our spiritual growth, including with each other. The aliens want our picture of reality to change at a very fundamental level. They are doing what is needed to help us to see the universe through different spiritual perspectives.

The Breeding Program

Some of the more recent material on UFO abductions suggests that the aliens are engaged in some sort of genetic engineering program for the purpose of creating human/alien hybrid offspring. I personally have never been exposed to this type of program or induced in any way to participate, but other people have reported these experiences.

Numerous women abductees have reported undergoing a variety of gynecological procedures, including egg harvesting, insemination, and removal of partial-term fetuses. Some women have suffered a variety of internal complications, including a high incidence of ovarian cysts, that are thought to be related to the procedures. Also linked to the UFO phenomenon are cases of "missing fetus syndrome," in which a pregnant woman's fetus mysteriously and inexplicably disappears overnight, without any indication of a miscarriage. And although I have never had the experience, male abductees report the forced collection of sperm.

Some contactees report being shown a baby and told that the baby is a hybrid, and that the abductee is the parent.

When I first ran across these reports, I didn't want to believe they were true. I like these beings and didn't want to view them as engaging in this kind of intrusive activity. It seemed like such a huge violation of peoples' physical space. However, I had to concede that there appeared to be strong evidence that these things have been done.

As much as I dislike what appears to be happening, such a procedure would make sense from a scientific perspective. The microenvironment of the human body seems to be of prime interest to the aliens. When a woman carries an embryo, that embryo is affected by the environment in the womb, maturing under the influence of human hormones and growth factors, and developing certain immunities and biochemical characteristics. Many of the antibodies that protect humans from the bacteria and viruses in our environment are developed in the fetus during the first trimester. For an adaptable species, it isn't too farfetched to think that placing an embryo inside a human host during its early developmental stages could give the embryo a much stronger tolerance for, and affinity to, the Earth's environment than it might otherwise have.

It's not clear if these fetuses were purely human or human/alien hybrids, or where the fetuses were ultimately taken. Nor do we know if this type of procedure is continuing in the present. The overwhelming majority of abductees who were shown babies describe these babies as listless and apathetic-looking. Whether the breeding program was an attempt at union that turned out to be a failure, we do not know.

It's possible that, in the future, hybrids will appear openly on the Earth. If so, our society may have great trouble dealing with it, especially if the hybrids' social systems and value systems differ radically from ours. My feeling is that the required paradigm shift would be challenging, but not impossible. After all, sixty years ago in South Africa, you could be killed for having sex with someone of a different race. Human perspectives do change. Given that we're dealing with the survival of humanity, there may be a lot of contextual shifts we'll have to undergo. Am I justifying these intrusive procedures (if they are, in fact, taking place)? No. I am saying that perhaps this is the way that things had to be done. I do know that, as a society, we're in for some hard transitions. This may be one of them.

Relationships

Over the years, I've come to understand that at the core of the abduction phenomenon is the aliens' struggle for a relationship. They want to know us and to understand us. During my initial physical contact experience in Winnipeg, the overpowering love that radiated from the being I was interacting with was unlike anything I'd ever experienced in human life. It was pure and all-encompassing, as if it came from God. Memories of this love helped me to confront the fear of later experiences. However, it's still been difficult to reconcile such incredible, unconditional love with the terror and physical discomfort that some of these experiences have caused. The aliens are so very, very different from us.

Perhaps the only analogy I can fall back on is that of the relationship between the rehab patient and the caregiver who is conducting the intervention. There will be sternness and unpleasantness when lessons must be learned, but there are opportunities to develop strong and caring relationships over time. Difficult as the contacts have been, they have opened up a world of new possibilities and left me with the inescapable feeling that the destinies of humanity and the aliens are intertwined.

The aliens build these relationships very carefully, with nothing left to chance. The contacts have been carefully orchestrated over my lifetime, planned and directed with purpose, each one designed to test and discover more about who I am, emotionally and psychologically. I believe there are many other people experiencing the same kind of intimate contact, carried out by the aliens with the same careful planning and purpose. Like myself, many of those abductees report struggling to come to terms with their experiences. Many report that once they are able to begin to feel a positive relationship with the aliens, it helps them to assimilate their experiences and develop a spiritual understanding and peace.

Sexual Aspects of Contact

Many contactees report a strongly sexual component to their experiences (as distinct from a medical component involving investigations of the reproductive system). Without going into too much detail, I will concur with this. It's common for contactees to perceive one being among the aliens to be of the opposite sex, and to feel, at times, a strong sexual affinity with that being. The depth of passion and sense of absolute union can far exceed those found in most human sexual relationships.

In my case, the affinity was pure and whole and very complete. There was no sense of anything bad about it, just an overwhelming sense of connectedness and union that embraced the whole being. There was a sense, when she was with me, that I knew her. She was no stranger, but someone that I knew well. The power of the experience was incredible. It was as if she was trying to understand and embrace everything about me, to fully share the experience and to know who I really was at my deepest level of being. This is one aspect of these contact relationships that many people do not yet understand: there is no stone that goes unturned regarding who you really are. At times, this intimacy of experience—not the sexual aspects of it, but the overall relationship—can create total terror. There is literally no place to hide any aspect of who you really are. They seem to look right into your soul.

Given this degree of connection, the sexual component becomes inevitable. Humans are sexual and spiritual beings, and if you really want to know somebody intimately, you have to share in their sexuality. Despite what society says, despite all the hang-ups that we are given or taught by society, the simple fact is that our sexuality is an important part of any intimate relationship, including the contact relationship. We can't get around it, and if we try to make it "bad," we are cheating our souls out of the full experience of communion.

There is such an incredible depth and complexity to the whole contact experience. No wonder people are struggling with it!

Other Manifestations of the Aliens: What's Real?

"Shattering our limited perceptual view of this reality will be surprisingly easy. However, the development of a greater human understanding of our true place in the Universe will be exceedingly difficult."

Crop circles, cattle mutilations, a crashed saucer in 1947—there is a vast body of folklore and conjecture surrounding the UFO phenomenon. In my opinion, many of these phenomena do not involve the aliens at all. As with other things in life, I could be wrong, but I disagree with other researchers on some major points. Very briefly, here are my perspectives on a few common issues.

Ancient Civilizations

By and large, science has done a fine job of proving that ancient structures, like the pyramids in Egypt and the statues on Rapa Nui (Easter Island), were built using technologies that those cultures developed by themselves. There are indications that technology was exchanged between Egypt and South America, but there is really no evidence that alien technology was involved. By contrast, there is fairly good evidence that many ancient civilizations evolved over periods of time, developed technology, and lost it as their societies collapsed. If there's one thing that's constant among all social systems, it's that they grow, flower, then collapse. And in the collapse, much information is lost.

Another reason I don't believe that the aliens have shared any sort of technology with us is that humanity is a fairly violent species, and has been for some time. In the same way that you don't hand a child a loaded weapon, the aliens have probably known better than to give us technology. This hypothesis is not a popular one with a large number of people currently in the field of UFO studies, but I stand by it.

Crop Circles?

There is increasing evidence that some crop circles are man-made (hoaxes), while the rest seem to be created naturally by twister-like wind vortices that touch down in crop fields. Nor do the crop circles fit with what we know about UFO landing sites.

In cases where we have reliable witness accounts of UFO landings, the sites generally exhibit burned or radioactive areas, and/or distinct small depressions that indicate that the craft landed on supporting legs. None of the crop circles I've ever heard about show any of these characteristics.

Another reason I don't believe that the aliens have anything to do with crop circles is that the circles have no discernible purpose that fits in with what the aliens are here to do. From my experience, if these beings want you to know they exist, their ways of introducing themselves are far more direct than making circles in cornfields.

Animal Mutilations?

My belief is that, although alien involvement in animal mutilations is not impossible, it's highly unlikely. The evidence is just not very strong. Although I'm no expert, all the cattle mutilations that I've seen could be explained in other ways. In some cases, I think we're dealing with cattle that died from normal causes and had predators feed on the carcasses before their discovery. Other mutilations have been faked.

My first question is: why would the aliens do it? The most common assertion is that mutilations are done to extract DNA. Why destroy an animal to take DNA? Why take out organs? One strand of hair will give anyone all the DNA they'll ever need.

One of the challenges of determining the true cause of animal mutilations is that they are not thoroughly investigated. This is not a negative reflection on researchers; even conscientious researchers operate with limited resources. Detailed forensic evaluation is time-consuming and expensive, and there isn't really much incentive or opportunity to do it.

I applaud the determination of anyone looking for answers, and I'd like to see the government put together a solid research team and collect evidence that can be reviewed objectively by everyone.

Roswell?

"The evidence points to the fact that Roswell was a real incident and that indeed an alien craft did crash, and that material was recovered from that site. We all know that UFOs are real. All we need to ask is where do they come from, and what do they want?"
—Edgar Dean Mitchell, former NASA astronaut; captain, United States Navy, Ret.

Many people who know nothing else about the UFO phenomenon have heard reports that a UFO crashed in Roswell, New Mexico, in July 1947, and that the US government recovered dead aliens and pieces of a ship.

Much about the incident is unclear. It's a matter of public record that local rancher William Brazel and his children discovered wreckage on their farm and contacted authorities. For some reason that was not divulged, Brazel was imprisoned for several days, then cautioned not to discuss the event for national security reasons. Initial announcements were made by the military to the effect that extraterrestrial material had been recovered, but these announcements were soon retracted in favor of a statement that the items discovered were, in fact, the wreckage of a weather balloon.

Years later, high-ranking military officials who had been at the Roswell site confirmed that the recovered materials—including a thin metal foil that could not be permanently deformed or damaged, and a light substance resembling balsa wood that would not burn—were not of Earthly origin. It was also confirmed that the US Air Force had initiated a disinformation campaign to obscure the truth. Some sources speculate that the craft exploded over

Roswell, shedding debris, but actually crashed at Socorro, New Mexico, after which a craft and alien bodies were recovered from that location by the air force and transmitted to Wright Patterson Air Force Base for storage. Years later, it was speculated that the air force had indeed been involved in a coverup—but not of UFO activity. Instead, the coverup allegedly involved the crash of a strategic defense device that originated either at Los Alamos or as part of the emerging US space program.

This is a perplexing problem because a crash of an alien craft would infer that the aliens were either unable or unwilling to recover the damaged craft and the bodies of their comrades. I guess this scenario is possible, but, remember, we're talking about beings who can float through walls and alter states of consciousness at will. Possibly they had fewer abilities sixty years ago or it was a different, less evolved, species, or they were still learning to manipulate effectively within our reality. The fact is that the technology I was exposed to was so overwhelmingly superior to ours that I can't find a good reason why they could not or would not recover their own comrades and craft. At any rate, it would have been a grievous error to allow any advanced technology to fall into the hands of any Earthly military power (good or bad), when the whole reason for the aliens' presence now appears to be our misuse of our own technology. Despite any misgivings, the excellent investigation and research conducted by Stanton Freidman gives strong weight to the argument that something alien in origin did in fact crash-land.

Regardless of my personal views (which change from time to time), I think we must applaud the efforts of everyone trying to uncover the truth about Roswell. With the work of a few dedicated professional researchers it's now undeniable that the incident has grown to near-mythical proportions. In doing so, it has galvanized public interest in the UFO phenomenon and public support for uncovering the truth—and that is always a good thing.

5

WHAT'S THEIR GOAL?

"Whatever nature has in store for mankind, unpleasant as it may be, men must accept, for ignorance is never better than knowledge."
—Enrico Fermi, Nobel Prize winner, nuclear physicist

Surprising as it may seem to some people, there is no real consensus within the UFO community as to what is happening. This isn't too hard to understand; in any area of science where humanity is on the forefront of new discoveries—medicine and astronomy are two examples—there is often a lack of consensus.

Many abductees report that during their abduction experiences, they are shown apocalyptic visions and warned telepathically that humanity is in crisis. Abductees may be shown wasted landscapes after a nuclear war or see environmental destruction and witness the Earth dying from pollution. Almost all abductees come to believe that humanity is in grave danger of its own design, and that a catastrophe of biblical proportions seems imminent.

I'm no exception. In one vision, I saw myself standing under a spaceship, dressed in a silvery one-piece suit. I had grey in my hair and weighed a little more, but of course I am not without my vanity. Once I recognized myself I was little relieved that I wasn't really overweight. Beside me stood a dark-haired woman who wore a similar suit, but I didn't recognize her. Suddenly a dark somber feeling began to well up within me. This was no dream, this was something different, this was something real. I was seeing some event in the future! In front of my older self and this woman stood a line of people of all ages and races dressed in casual clothes, all strangers to one another. A young girl of thirteen years was holding a baby who was not hers. It seemed that we were organizing them to enter into the ship. There was light under the ship, but it seemed oppressively dark everywhere outside the landing area. I could sense many people and feelings of fear and confusion that seemed to extend for hundreds of miles in all directions.

The feeling that permeated everything could only be described as grim. One might consider such feelings as odd, bearing in mind that we were apparently being moved to safety. Consider how you would respond to leaving everything you worked for all your life, all your passions, your home, all your friends, all your family, all your children, all your loved ones. What if you also knew that those left behind would suffer terribly and likely never be seen again. How would you really feel? Lucky? Relieved? I certainly didn't experience those emotions and I pray to God that day never has to come.

Although it's possible that some of these catastrophic visions are shown to contactees as psychological tests designed to evaluate the response of the individual, the effect on contactees is so profound that it almost invariably evokes a new level of concern for the Earth. A leading African Sansui (high-level medicine man) once explained of his contact experiences that "I am shown that the world is dying . . . the thing you are looking into is real. It is not a figment of anyone's imagination. . . ." To many contactees, the sadness triggered by these visions can be almost overwhelming. Experiencing the visions is not like looking at a film; you feel completely immersed in the experiences and their attendant emotions.

These visions give us a key clue as to why the aliens are here. As previously mentioned, the aliens are here to help us rethink our relationship to the technology we have created. The visions are their way of showing us the dangers we're facing. Unlike humans, who rely on words, the aliens have the capacity to link directly to other minds and transmit images that convey information in a far more visceral form. The recipient not only comprehends the message, but *experiences* it at a very fundamental level.

From a spiritual point of view, our world is covered in darkness. We have separated ourselves from our creator and from each other. It's entirely possible that we threaten not only ourselves, but other living beings in other dimensions. If we're to understand what actions we need to take, we need to take a hard look at exactly what we've done.

War

"Wars may sometimes be a necessary evil. But no matter how necessary, it is always an evil, never a good. We will not learn to live in peace by killing each other's children."
—Jimmy Carter

It's no coincidence that the aliens began to make their presence known around the same time the first atomic bomb was created. Many abductees have suggested that the aliens are here to help us survive a global crisis linked to nuclear war.

There is a great deal to be concerned about. One study made about twenty years ago by the World Health Organization indicated that a nuclear war between the United States and Russia could kill one billion people outright. It could also produce a nuclear winter that would probably kill an additional one billion people. In other words, it's possible that about one-third of all the people on Earth would be wiped out almost immediately by global thermonuclear war, and the rest would be reduced to a state of prolonged agony and chaos.

It becomes clear why the aliens are so interested in observing and understanding military development, as evidenced by the numerous UFO sightings around military installations and airports. This of course has had a correspondingly negative response from the military. They must consider the phenomenon a possible threat and treat it as such. Despite what the military may think, the aliens are not assessing our defenses with a view to overwhelming those defenses. They simply want to assess our ever-increasing ability to destroy ourselves.

As more and more countries develop nuclear weapons and nuclear energy programs, the situation becomes increasingly grim. However, I don't think the solution will be as simplistic as getting together and saying, "No nuclear weapons for anybody." Nuclear weapons are only a by-product of human fear and the current human need to dominate. If the aliens vaporized every nuclear weapon tomorrow, we'd simply find other methods of killing people. Some basic spiritual development is needed if the world is going to move into an era of real peace.

The way our society is structured right now, nobody can escape the military mind-set. If you want a country, you'd better have an army. If you don't have a strong army, you'd better know someone who does. But again, it's far too simplistic to say that if we suddenly stop fighting, the problem will be solved. Right now, there are some very courageous people who are fighting, and dying, to try to build better lives for their fellow humans. These are difficult times, and the answers are not clear. However, one thing I *am* convinced of is that the aliens have a much broader perspective on the whole issue, and we would do well to open ourselves to their insights.

It's significant that the aliens haven't come down to Earth and said, "We're going to talk to your leaders," or, "We're going to take away all your weapons." Instead, they are interacting with ordinary individuals all around the world. Maybe there's a clue in that. Maybe the solution will be born through individual people refusing to participate in the nonsense that's going on. Maybe we have confused compassion with tolerance, and we simply need to start saying that we, as a society and a species, will no longer allow actions that are harmful to others. Maybe those who will survive will be able to build an enhanced, more harmonious world. Maybe the armies of the future will be composed of people willing to give their lives for real peace, without the use of weapons.

The Environment

Just like our problems with war, humanity's growing environmental problems are an indirect result of our spiritual defects.

It may have been easier to link with our environment and understand its mystical harmonies when we were hunter-gatherers. Our lives depended upon it. But as we began to move to urban areas, most of us became desensitized to our environment. It became increasingly difficult to spiritually connect to our environment on a daily basis.

The connection between the environment and war is clear: if you degrade and pollute your living space to the point that it will no longer sustain you, you will be forced to find a new living space. If that space belongs to others, you will be tempted to seize it by force if you have to. Is it any wonder why so many people think that aliens also have these motives? After all, it is a story that played out many times throughout human history. Yet, doesn't it seem more sensible that advanced, self-aware life-forms must learn to live in harmony with their environment and with each other?

The connection between overpopulation and war is equally clear. If you overpopulate, you use more resources. If you overuse the resources in your area, you will be compelled to take resources from others. If you are unable to seize or create sufficient resources, your standard of living will degrade and great portions of the population may perish.

We have overpopulated the Earth in some areas and over-worked its resources, making territorial fighting inevitable. And given our current technological capacities, it would not take much to tip the balance and spiral out of control. However, when we increase education and standards of living, the population growth naturally stabilizes.

Clearly the aliens should not consider giving us more advanced technology that could be misused. It's not their goal to help us perpetuate our degradation and mismanagement of Mother Earth. They should want us to stay right here and put our own house in order. We have become spiritually separated from our planet and all the other living things on it. They want us to face that, and solve it.

The great spiritual leaders of the world believe that our hopes for peace and survival depend on our ability to develop sufficient spiritual maturity to defuse an impending ecological, or human, catastrophe.

We may fail. It's entirely possible that the medical procedures being undergone by contactees are intended to help them survive a change in macroenvironment, be it disease, pollution, or high levels of nuclear radiation. In other words, the aliens may be preparing us for the worst. We just don't know.

One of the unexpected feelings that these contacts have generated is grief. Grief that we're probably going to screw this world up very badly before we find a way to fix it. Grief for all the suffering and deaths that humanity is most likely going to experience before we learn how to stop damaging the planet and each other.

The only silver lining is that I believe that humanity will save itself, but it will depend upon your actions in the end. The outcome will be close—very, very close. I believe that we will make it, but we will need a lot of good people to make sure that happens. This intervention could also be described as the power of the Creator at work. The aliens have shown a great sense of urgency and concern.

Why Don't They Just Take Over?

Right after 9/11, my daughter asked me, "If the aliens are here to help us, why didn't they do anything to prevent that (pointing to the horrific pictures on TV) from happening?"

It was an honest, heartfelt question born of concern about man's inhumanity to man. But when you really think about it, why should the aliens physically intervene to help us? This is our world, not theirs. My daughter's question is really a variation of: if God is really up there, why does He (or She or It) allow good people to be hurt? The intent behind the question is understandable, but many of us know that God doesn't intervene in that fashion. The classic explanation is that the Creator gave us free will and we are supposed to use it to improve the world.

Regardless of your personal beliefs, achieving a peaceful world is up to us. It would be a terrible mistake to start looking at the alien beings as our saviors. They can try to help us and to open up new paths for us to take, but they aren't here to assume control. We have to do the work ourselves. This principle also applies on a personal level. I'm sure that the aliens have the ability to fix my knee problems and other sports injuries, but they haven't done it. I've still got to assume responsibility for my own well-being: see the doctor, live with pain, and struggle for a healthy physical and emotional life. Having contact is not a shortcut to solving your personal challanges.

How Might Change Happen?

Humanity has to be ready for wholesale change. Unless we're motivated, there will be no change. At this point, there are not enough of us who are sufficiently motivated. Maybe we need an event so raw and so devastating that it shocks us into readiness. I hope such a thing won't happen, but it might. Sometimes people are only motivated to change when they've lost everything: their house, their car, their food, everything. This is why I say that the process is not going to be easy. As painful as it would be, we may see billions of people dying before humanity comes to the point of saying, "This isn't working. Let's find another way."

There is of course a historical precedent for humanity to have a desire to find a lasting world peace. It happened after two world wars and resulted in the formation of the League of Nations and later the United Nations. Arguably both have failed in achieving their original vision, but we should not discount the effort that was made.

Whatever happens, the changes we make will not heal our problems overnight. The repercussions on humanity are going to be felt for a long, long time. We're going to destroy a lot of ourselves unnecessarily, destroy a lot of what we have today.

Likely the aliens will eventually show themselves openly in such a way that their existence can't be denied. I don't believe they will suddenly appear to all humanity at a point of time when there is a great single catastrophe. It's more likely that they will continue with their current strategy of contact, and appear gradually to all humanity during a series of major events.

It's unclear what the actual change point will be. Likely it will be some kind of domino effect; certain factors will line up and the dominoes will start falling. The dominoes may involve major incidents with governments or political systems, epidemics, some sudden ecological disaster, or other factors. It will probably be much like the global warming phenomenon. Many of the pieces were known for years, but it took the UN report on climate change to start the dominoes falling in a way that forced governments to respond.

What's inevitable is that changes are coming. We need to seriously consider how we should be preparing to deal with the aliens, the coming crises, and the transitions that will result.

What Can We Do?

"I believe governments fear that if they did disclose those facts, people would panic. I don't believe that at all. There is a serious possibility that we are being visited by people from outer space. It behooves us to find out who they are, where they come from, and what they want."
—John Callaghan, senior FAA official of accidents and investigations

Now that we understand the probable shape of the future, there are three key areas involved in planning our response:

personal spirituality, government, and science. The starting point for change must be personal spirituality. Ultimately, it's a person's beliefs that drive his or her opinions and actions. Taken collectively, the opinions and actions of everyone within a society constitute *public opinion*, which, in a democratic society, is a major driver of government policy and action. Government policy, in turn, has a major effect on scientific funding and social programs.

The change paradigm can therefore be seen as a pyramid. At its base lie the personal spirituality and beliefs of innumerable individuals. These combine to form public opinion—the priorities of the society as a whole. Government, acting on these priorities, then creates the policies and social programs to yield the desired results. Thus, personal spirituality is the first step in a chain of events that ultimately creates social progress.

6

SPIRITUALITY

"Our fearful and aggressive response to the ET presence
is understandable and even predicable. In many ways it's
a sad reflection of our world's problems and humanity's
present state of spiritual development, or rather lack of it!"
—Jim Moroney

Lieutenant Milton Torres was based in Britain when he received the order: "Get up there, arm all weapons, and fire on sight." He scrambled into his military Saber fighter aircraft and soared into the air to meet an unknown threat. He observed and reported a craft larger than an aircraft carrier traveling at mach 10+. He knew instinctively it was a UFO and not of this world. Mr. Torres is now a retired professor of civil engineering living in Miami and explained that the day after he was scrambled from RAF Manston he received a visit from an American in a trench coat who waved a National Security Agency identity card at him and warned him that, if he ever revealed what had happened, he would never fly again.

The most troubling aspect of this account was that he was ordered to fire upon a UFO! Now let's lean back in our comfortable armchairs and contemplate this strategic directive. We have an alien craft that enters Earth's atmosphere. Its interplanetary journey probably means that the crew will consist of family units including males, females, and children. Of course this is just speculation, but our first friendly gesture would be to shoot their asses out of the sky and murder the lot of them! Mr. Torres had a deep-seated feeling that what he was told to do was going to have enormous consequences. To his astonishment and relief the object rapidly moved out of sight and range of his weapons.

If spiritual starvation were a disease, the human race would be considered terminally ill. Despite our general feelings of wellness, we are much sicker than we realize.

Human beings are, in essence, spiritual beings, but we have forgotten that. Most of us have been taught to place a high premium on intelligence, but we don't truly understand what intelligence means. We think that intelligence is all about being smart: having a good memory, being able to solve problems, and so on. However, without a deep understanding of the *ramifications* of our actions, we are not truly intelligent. To be truly intelligent, we must learn to understand the consequences of our actions within the context of the whole living universe. True intelligence is directly linked to spiritual consciousness. It bears repeating that the aliens do not perceive themselves as better than us. They simply have a greater spiritual understanding and sense of connection to the Creator.

Whether or not the goal of the aliens is to stimulate our spiritual development, it appears that individual contactees must experience some sort of spiritual development in order to come to full terms with their contact experiences. The human mind seeks understanding. It demands it. These encounters are too strange and too overpowering to simply ignore or dismiss. I do not believe that the human psyche could survive for long under the belief that the universe was a disordered nightmare where inexplicable phenomena could come crashing through the barriers of reality at any time. For their own peace of mind, contactees are forced to try and understand these experiences.

If this process of understanding is a journey, then North Americans embark on it from the worst possible point of origin. We have separated the scientific from the spiritual and locked them into separate compartments. My own experience was no exception. Not only was I raised under the accepted North American concepts of reality, my profession involved the practice of science. Reality was to be understood by repeatable experiments and objective proof, filtered through the known laws of physics.

People who haven't had contact with aliens often underestimate the difficulties involved in assimilating these experiences. There are people who've said to me in complete earnestness, "I really wish I could have an experience with an extraterrestrial or something." *Be careful what you wish for.* It's not like sitting down over coffee and fruitcake to discuss a bit of politics and philosophy. These experiences rock your psyche right to its core. It's not just that the aliens can be intrusive, difficult, and demanding. The interaction often feels like the ground of reality begins to liquefy under your feet as your conceptual understanding of this world is almost completely destroyed.

Rebuilding takes time, and spiritual growth seems to be the key. Researchers have found that many contactees only start to assimilate their experiences after they begin to develop a spiritual perspective. As the contactee develops a heightened environmental consciousness and an awareness of the importance of all life, these new perspectives seem to help that person integrate the unpleasant and terrifying elements of the abduction experience. Abductees begin to feel that their experiences were for a purpose and have an overall positive meaning. They come to believe that the experiences have deepened their consciousness and helped them to better connect with themselves and the universe. Although this deep transformation has been reported only in people who have worked intensively with their experiences in nonordinary states of consciousness, it's quite possible that other abductees have had spontaneous spiritual growth and transformation, and have thus not felt the need to seek therapy.

There is often a relationship between trauma and spiritual growth. In ordinary human life, spiritual growth is frequently triggered by traumatic experiences. Many cultures make use of this fact by imposing spiritual disciplines or coming-of-age rites that include harsh practices that are designed to stimulate spiritual development. The rituals are carefully conducted to trigger changes in the initiate's self-appraisal and worldview.

It's possible that the fear and trauma generated by the contact experience are somehow helping us to evolve spiritually, so we can help to reconstruct our relationship with this world. Some contactees, including myself, believe that before we came into this lifetime, we chose the difficult path of interaction with these beings. It's as if, over many lifetimes, we have had numerous opportunities to change but have failed to do so. Our role in the contact phenomenon is our test of ourselves.

If we're to succeed, it will be useful to understand the whole process of spiritual growth in more detail. In particular, we need to know if there are ways to initiate spiritual growth at will, without the associated trauma.

What Does Spiritual Development Look Like?

"All major religious traditions carry basically the same message, that is love, compassion and forgiveness . . . the important thing is they should be part of our daily lives."
—The Dalai Lama

Classical Western psychology has done a wonderful job of exploring and defining psychological illness; however, it has not worked particularly hard at exploring the components of spiritual development or spiritual health. First, let's clarify what is meant by spirituality and its relationship to human life. In this book, spirituality is defined as an awareness of, and respect for, the life around us, and a commitment to acting with respect for life. Under this definition, spirituality must necessarily be beneficial both to the individual and to society.

There is no recipe for spiritual development; however, there are models that we can follow. Eastern philosophy has spent thousands of years trying to define what makes people psychologically healthy. More recently, there has emerged a Western field of psychology that holds real promise for helping us understand and explore the contact phenomenon. This is the field of *transpersonal psychology*.

Although transpersonal psychology recognizes that psychological illness exists, it does not, as practitioners like Freud have done, derive its basic model of human consciousness by studying the ill or diseased psyche. Instead, transpersonal psychology focuses on psychological health and human potential. It views individuals as being engaged in a continuous process of transformation and development toward full humanity. Transpersonal psychology approaches the individual as a whole person and seeks a balanced development of the intellectual, emotional, spiritual, physical, social, and creative aspects of life. In seeking to understand how spiritual growth occurs, transpersonal psychology draws on the best of a variety of existing spiritual practices, including traditional psychology, meditation, yoga, and other ancient transformative and healing practices. To explore this field, I enrolled with the Institute of Transpersonal Psychology in 1998. The studies were invaluable in helping me gain personal spiritual perspective and understand how transpersonal psychology could be applied to the abduction phenomenon.

Much has been written about the specific spiritual practices used in transpersonal psychology, so this book will not delve deeply into that information. Instead, we'll try to characterize what a rapid spiritual development might look like.

Many cultures have described energy systems within the body and used these energy systems as the foundation for medical treatments. Spiritual evolution is often accompanied by—or stimulated by—changes in energy flow within these systems. These changes may be induced by illness, spiritual practice, or unplanned trauma. As energy flow changes, consciousness changes. Characteristic of rapid spiritual evolution are a wide variety of experiences that involve the consciousness, including out-of-body experiences, psychic experiences, powerful dreams, etc. It's as if the nervous system and psyche are literally operating in a new fashion and learning new "rules of the road." It's notable that other societies that are more open to the idea of altered states of consciousness and spirit beings have a much easier time accepting the contact phenomenon.

Spiritual experiences are not always glorious revelations. They can be a far cry from the idealized situation where an angel floats into the room and gently taps you on the head to confer wisdom. Instead, they can be bewildering, forceful, and even traumatic. For example, when I was in my early thirties, I had an experience where I started seeing auras. It was late one afternoon when I began feeling tremors of energy surging through my body. About an hour later the shaking finally stopped and I was able to discern a faint type of colored glow around most objects. It was certainly distressing. All kinds of wild thoughts went through my head. Was it a brain tumor? Was it some kind of nervous system disorder? What the hell was happening? When the shaking finally subsided, not only could I see auras, but everything around me seemed more vibrant and colorful. It was almost as if I had been watching life in black-and-white and had suddenly switched to color vision.

In spite of the vibrancy, it was disconcerting to suddenly perceive the physical world differently than I had just an hour earlier. And it made small, but unexpected, changes in my world. For example, one of my friends was a smoker. To see if he was home, I used to look at the crack under his door, because if he was there you could usually see faint signs of smoke in the air. After I started seeing auras, I saw so much residual glow from the auras of the door and the door frame that it masked any signs of smoke. From that point on, I always had to knock on his door to see if he was home. I don't pay much attention to the auras now, but at the time, I found it difficult to adjust.

How Does This Relate to the Contact Phenomenon?

Since at least part of the reason that the aliens are here is to initiate a rapid spiritual development in humans, it makes sense that reading about the experiences of others, and understanding the philosophy of spiritual development, will be invaluable to abductees looking for guidance. The information may also help equip them to cope with possible spiritual emergencies that might occur as a result of their continued contact experiences.

Transpersonal psychology, with its emphasis on spiritually transformative processes and their manifestations (telepathy, clairvoyance, etc.), seems uniquely suited to this role. Many contactees have reported perceptions of increased clairvoyance, telepathy, and other psychic manifestations, combined with an increased general awareness of the importance of all life. Transpersonal psychology gives contactees a framework for assimilating these experiences. (Whether or not contactees' claims are object-ively verifiable, it's certain that they feel an increased sense of con-nection to the world around them. It's difficult to see how that could be anything but beneficial. We tend not to rob, assault, lie to, or otherwise harm those whom we feel truly connected to.)

Upsetting as the contact experiences and the resulting spirit-ual evolutions can be, individuals can emerge with a greater sense of self, and a greater sense of peace. My own experience con-firms this. I don't hate the aliens for the frightening experiences and painful medical procedures that I've undergone. Instead, I've come to see these experiences as part of the heavy price that must be paid in order to give all of us a chance.

Someone once asked me if the alien beings ever hurt me. They were looking for some way to categorize them as good or bad. That type of logic has some fatal flaws. I don't hate my den-tist, although I've never found dental work particularly pleasant or pain free. In fact there are few intrusive medical procedures that don't involve some form of discomfort. I certainly don't con-sider any of my doctors or dentists as bad people because they hurt me. I am certainly willing to accept pain if I believe it is in my personal best interest or in the interest of others.

Many contactees develop a sense of shared responsibility for the state of the world that is difficult to explain to someone who does not have that perspective. Perhaps we simply feel that if we want to make the world a better place, we need to start with our-selves. Ultimately, it is a trust relationship. Most people who have had repeated contact experiences come to feel that the aliens truly represent the unconditional love and communion that emanate from God—a God who doesn't want anyone burned at the stake, or killed for their beliefs, or harmed in any way. It's a feeling I'm inclined to trust.

What Does This Mean for Society?

As a society, we need to move past our fixation on technology and start thinking about what an advanced social structure might look like. It's vital to remember that spiritual advancement does not mean an absence of suffering, pain, or sacrifice. There will still be tough choices to make, even in a spiritually aware culture. Spirituality will not eliminate confrontations, nor will spirituality be perceived as sitting on a log and doing nothing. Spirituality will be active. The actual shape of a spiritually advanced human culture will certainly be different from our culture today.

It's difficult to comprehend how the aliens will be able to stimulate deep and profound changes in our social structure and spiritual natures without provoking the collapse of our current culture. Our best course of action will probably only become clear after we've endured a series of really bad times. Unfortunately, I have no solutions, but I know we had better start looking. We will need the courage to build a bridge of understanding and accept the aliens' invitation to walk down a new road.

What Will Happen to Religion?

"Extraterrestrial contact is a real phenomenon. The Vatican is receiving much information about extraterrestrials and their contacts with humans from its nuncios (embassies) in various countries, such as Mexico, Chile and Venezuela."
—Monsignor Corrado Balducci, Vatican theologian and insider close to the Pope

People are inherently spiritual beings and they generally like to come together to share that communion. In that sense, there's nothing wrong with organized religion. Most religions are not inherently bad—it's specific individuals within religions that make things bad by choosing to focus on certain extreme aspects of that religion's teachings. However, within our religious systems there are some very good people who have helped humanity to evolve spiritually.

Most of the major religions have at some time promoted violence as an undertone to their teachings. Others have isolated themselves as "chosen" and special in the eyes of their God. As we evolve spiritually toward true peace, the kind of sectarian approach that promotes superiority and violence within a context of "God's will" is going to have to disappear. There will simply be no place for it. Religions are made up of individuals and shaped by those individuals. As true spirituality develops, it's unlikely that human beings will continue to support religions that think in terms of establishing dominion over others.

As human spiritual development proceeds, religions will be forced to evolve. Religious leaders will struggle with that. The religions that are most flexible will probably have the best chance of keeping their followers and surviving with some of their belief structures intact. It seems unlikely that some new kind of religion will spring up, but it wouldn't be surprising to see certain religious leaders attempt to cast the aliens in the role of a new threat. I'm optimistic that such an attempt would ultimately fail and that the majority of world religions will be open to a greater reality.

I'm not in favor of aggressively dismantling all the world religions, nor am I in favor of building cults to promote the newest spiritual leader from this or any other world. I am in favor of individuals making sane, reasonable choices that result in long-term benefits for themselves, those around them, and the environment in which they live.

How Education Might Change

"I know nothing except the fact of my ignorance."
—Socrates

It's likely that the way we educate young people will change dramatically. I think we'll put more emphasis on educating our children about who they are and what life is really all about, and about more productive ways of dealing with conflict. (Of course, we first need to discover those answers. If the majority of us really knew these things, humanity wouldn't be in the pickle that it's in.) There are children in our world who are being raised to kill. We have always had children who have been raised to kill. We've raised generations of people for war and conflict. The question now becomes: how do we raise people for peace? I think we can accomplish this, because love comes more naturally than hate. If you can teach people to hate, you should be able to teach them to love. We need to start educating people about love—how to truly love themselves and their enemies. We need to start educating people against war, against aggression, and against subjugation of any kind. I believe we can have a creative, dynamic culture of individuals without having the fear of war. Perhaps in the future we'll still have armies and people who are willing to sacrifice their lives for peace, but not armies as we know them today. Maybe we will have armies without weapons, but with individuals who are willing to undergo individual sacrifice for peace.

A Final Word on Spirituality

I cannot overstress the idea that any spiritual work that people choose to do *must not* take precedence over their lives and relationships in the here-and-now. Real life is not somewhere "out there" on the aliens' ships. Real life is here on Earth, today. Any changes that we make must directly benefit our lives and the lives of those around us.

7

GOVERNMENT

"Many government officials prefer to be ignorant of the UFO phenomenon. They don't know because they don't want to know!"
—Jim Moroney

Precautionary Principle in Science

In cases where scientific evidence appears contradictory, the precautionary principle demands that we move toward some form of action when the risks of doing something outweigh the risks of doing nothing.

There is a mountain of excellent scientific evidence to support the hypothesis that we are being contacted by extraterrestrials and very little to suggest we are not. It also feels like this intervention is being imposed upon the human race, but we are far from powerless. We can respond to the aliens' actions with changes of our own. Government could play a key role in this process. A government can make the entire process vastly easier—or infinitely more difficult—for its citizens.

It's not terribly productive to criticize governments for what's gone on in the past. What's done is done. However, if you want to *change* someone's behavior, the first step is always to understand *why* the person or organization has acted the way it has. Therefore, it's fruitful to start this chapter by discussing what kind of information governments are likely to have, and why they have responded to that information in the way they have. After that, we'll explore some constructive actions that governments might take in response to the emerging contact phenomenon.

What Do Governments Know?

"The phenomenon of UFOs does exist, and it must be treated seriously!"
—Mikhail Gorbachev, Nobel Peace Prize winner and former leader of the Soviet Union

A number of governments around the world have given in to public pressure and have begun to release their UFO reports and files. The Canadian government has authorized open public access to thousands of federal government documents concerning UFOs. By January 2009 a total of 9,500 digitized documents spanning the years 1947 to the early 1980s had been made available through the Library and Archives Canada website. Titled "Canada's UFOs: The Search for the Unknown," the files include correspondence, reports, memos, and procedures, some of which specifically deal with UFOs. The files come from Canada's National Defense Department, the Department of Transport, the National Research Council, and the Royal Canadian Mounted Police. The online release of its UFO X-files followed the release at the end of January 2009 of Denmark's UFO files. In a program started in May 2007, Great Britain continues to release thousands of UFO files. The French Space Agency announced on March 22, 2007, that it was making public its secret UFO files through a government website. One must wonder how much longer the United States will remain silent and when and how it will address the release of information.

It's reasonable to assume that most nations possessing nuclear weapons capabilities have some knowledge of the extraterrestrial phenomenon. Certainly, in each nation that is actively engaged in space exploration, there will be individuals within the space agencies or that nation's military or government who are aware of the extraterrestrials. As discussed in chapter 2, the United States discovered their existence in the early stages of the space program. In response, NASA, or whoever was making the decisions for NASA, simply decided to keep the evidence under wraps.

It's important to remember that in Westernized countries and most superpower countries, the government and the military are two distinct entities. The drawback to this state of affairs is that, in many cases, the people who make social policy—i.e., the government—are unaware of important information that the military is privy to. This isn't particularly hard to understand. Governments change, often every few years, and it doesn't really benefit the military to share high-level information with politicians who may only be in power for a few years. Because of this, there are limits to what our politicians know about the extraterrestrial phenomenon.

Some governments are aware of some of the evidence, and some scientists are aware, but we can't jump to too many negative conclusions. For example, I don't believe that anyone within the Canadian Parliament or the United States Senate has been briefed on the extraterrestrial presence.

Still, there are some good people within government. There are good politicians who are genuinely trying to do the best for their people. I don't believe it's productive to start attacking, blaming, or berating all government officials or military officials for what has or has not been done in the past. Let's work on educating them on what is happening now.

What Does the Military Fear?

*"There is strong evidence that all major policy decisions regarding
the UFO phenomenon have been made solely by the military
without consultation with elected officials or the public."*
—Jim Moroney

In a sense, I can sympathize with the predicament of NASA
and the military elements of many countries who do know about
the extraterrestrial presence, because they have no idea what they're
looking at. Understandably, they're reluctant to divulge the existence of a phenomenon that they have no understanding of, and
absolutely no power over. Not good for public confidence, perhaps?

From a military point of view, knowledge is often power. The
military simply has no incentive to reveal the things it does know.
There are no political advantages, so why do it? The military is not
in the business of informing people about anything. From a human
perspective, politicians and scientists have every reason in the world
to share this kind of information, because they have a duty to the
people and to the pursuit of knowledge. The military has no such
mandate. At the most basic level, it's supposed to keep secrets.

It's likely that military agencies around the world perceive the
aliens as a probable threat. To a military mind, any party or group
that has the technological ability to outmaneuver or disarm your best
technology must therefore be perceived as a possible threat. Whether
or not the aliens appear to be friendly is irrelevant. Any party that
can enter into protected military airspace at will and leave at will
(as the aliens have repeatedly done) must be perceived as a possible
threat and treated as such. To the military mind, if an entity has the
capacity to cause harm, it must be seen as a potential threat. Friend
or foe? In this context, the question is beside the point.

There are, in fact, indications that the aliens have interacted
with military technology. For example, in 1989, IKI (the Institute of Space Research of the Russian Academy of Sciences, the

Soviet equivalent of NASA) sent the *Phobos II* spacecraft to Mars to take photographs. The project was partially funded by private organizations. Shortly after reaching Mars, *Phobos II* stopped transmitting and disappeared. Naturally, the investors wanted to know what had happened. It was finally revealed that the almost-final photos of Mars that were transmitted from the satellite showed the shadow of an unknown object on the planet's surface. The shadow was elliptical in shape and roughly 16 miles long. Expert analysis of the photos concluded that it was the shadow of an unknown object hovering above the planet. The object was not, to the best of the Russian space agency's knowledge, supposed to be there. It was not another satellite. The very last photos transmitted by the *Phobos II* satellite have never been officially released. Some sources say that the pictures showed a long, almost straw-like object approach the satellite just before the satellite's transmissions stopped. The satellite itself was never recovered. If the *Phobos II* satellite had been fully government-owned, with no investors clamoring for answers, the truth might never have come out.

Other satellites have experienced problems as well. In 1993, the US Mars Observer probe stopped transmitting on arrival at Mars, and in spite of conjecture by NASA that its fuel tanks exploded, its fate is still unknown. In the late 1990s, a satellite being deployed by NASA at the end of a flexible tether (interestingly enough, it's rumoured that the Australian company that built the satellite and the tether called it "the Terminating Tether") was temporarily lost when the tether inexplicably snapped during deployment. When NASA retrieved the satellite, it didn't seem to have sustained any physical damage, but it did appear that its programming had been altered or interfered with. To the military mind, this kind of thing must be fairly worrisome. Who's interfering with these satellites, and why? If we send crews out into space, will they be interfered with as well?

The aliens have also interacted with the military in locations much closer to home. Robert Hastings, a UFO researcher, has done much to shed light on the attitudes of the military toward the extraterrestrials. Hastings has reported interviewing "literally dozens" of former and retired security team members who have been involved in numerous sightings of UFOs around nuclear installations and missile test sites. The interviews have uncovered some fascinating information. Hastings has reported that in many cases, witnesses testified that while the UFOs were in the vicinity of missile sites, the missile systems lost all electrical power. In one case, a missile system had no power for a full twenty-four hours, despite all attempts by utility personnel to restore power. Finally, for no discernible reason, the power system resumed normal operation. There are similar accounts of power outages over Russian military installations during UFO sightings.

The military's secrecy becomes immediately understandable: if there were times when your country's defense systems became undeployable, would you want anyone to know about it?

There are more mundane considerations as well. Given that NASA and the military operate within a very hierarchical "take me to your leader" type of structure, they really don't know how to respond to the alien presence. What can they do? Send out an emissary? Surprise: the aliens aren't interested in formal emissaries from countries. They're too busy talking to short-order cooks, farmers, writers, plumbers, and hundreds of other ordinary folk whom they've chosen to contact. The aliens are setting the agenda, and the military and NASA don't know how to work with that. (It's intriguing to speculate on whether the aliens ever did try to go through "official channels," only to conclude that if the official response was denial and coverup, they had better take their case directly to the people. Unfortunately, we may never know.)

We live in a military world. Humanity has put itself into

the situation where we need armies to protect countries, and as a result, many of our decisions are being made from military standpoints. Our military is very good at thinking in terms of protecting us from possible threats. That's its job, and by and large, it does it effectively.

Unfortunately, the mentality of many military organizations (and governments and societies) is very much concerned with domination. Who's on top? If it appears that the aliens are technologically superior, then to such a mind, the natural question is going to be, "Will they try to dominate us?" After all, we've got a long history of trying to dominate others. Military superpowers like to set the terms at the table. Clearly, the aliens are monitoring our military development, and just as clearly, our military will *not* be setting the terms of any interaction between the two parties. No wonder the military is uneasy.

There are many other theories as to why the military doesn't want people to know the truth. One of these is the "panic" theory, the idea being that if we tell people that the aliens are real, there will be mass panic. I'm skeptical. During one of my university extension classes, I asked my students how many of them were familiar with the subject of UFOs. (The class was a large, fairly diverse group of people who were probably a fairly good representation of society as a whole.) They all raised their hands. I asked why, if governments had proof that extraterrestrials were real, would they not tell the public?

"Because people would panic," one student said.

"Okay," I replied, "How many of you believe that people would panic?" About 90 percent of the class put up their hands.

"Okay," I said, "Which of you think you might panic?"

No one raised their hand! In fact, the theory that people would panic is not supported by any scientific data! There is abundant scientific evidence that demonstrates that public panic is rare, and most rare when people have been candidly informed.

Let's take this a step further. I personally don't believe there will be a problem with panic, but let's look at the issue on a purely hypothetical basis. Which alternative will make people *less* likely to panic: a deliberate, thoughtfully crafted announcement by a well-prepared government that is ready to put resources towards the problem—or a sudden and unexpected event that brings them face to face with the reality of the extraterrestrial presence and the fact that their government has lied to them?

In my experience, the aliens have shown the ability to break through into our individual worlds any time they choose. I don't think we can shield anyone from the truth by ignoring the phenomenon or disbelieving it. All we can do is make the process harder for everyone by marginalizing those who report UFOs or experience encounters. Conversely, if we accept, investigate with open minds, and plan based on what we find, it's reasonable to assume that we can make the process easier for all concerned.

The Space Program: UFO Research in Disguise

It becomes increasingly clear that the driving force behind the space program is not science, per se. Many, many people have pointed out that the actual benefits from the space station are out of all proportion to the costs. If you argue the need for space exploration in terms of scientific benefits, it doesn't make a lot of sense. However, if you accept the presence of the aliens, the space program makes perfect sense.

The driving force behind the space program is national security. The space program is the military's way of getting out there to see what it can find out about the extraterrestrials without arousing suspicions or having to publicly spill the beans about the extraterrestrial presence. Forget about growing plants in zero gravity; the space program is mostly about the military's attempt to investigate the extraterrestrials. Unfortunately most, if not all, of the information is going to be restricted as a result.

It's a strange feeling to see the astronomers focusing so strongly on finding planets that might support alien life. Sentient non-human life is here with us, right now. Yet we have these irrelevant investigations going on. Clearly, there is a fracture within the scientific community. It's been clear for some time that there are areas considered "appropriate" for public scientific funding, and areas that are not. Perhaps this is because private scientists funded by grants might expose the truth, whereas military scientists can be silenced by nondisclosure provisions. So the meaningful research is being done by the military, while the civilian scientists are off looking for intelligent life a couple of million light years away.

To me, this is one of the sad tragedies of twenty-first-century space exploration. The public is being told that tax dollars are needed to look for any hint that life can exist somewhere else in the universe. True, perhaps, as far as it goes, but billions of public dollars are being spent on purposes that the public knows nothing about. It's naïve to believe that the military has not built and launched satellites in an attempt to gather military intelligence on the location and activities of the extraterrestrials. There surely must be a significant amount of funding for such activities.

The Problem with Secrecy

"A decision to restrict information on the UFO phenomenon for the purpose of controlling it, when you have no control over it, defies all common sense. The outcomes of such appalling short-sighted decisions are as predictable as they will be catastrophic."
—Jim Moroney

If you're an autocratic government or military organization, secrets can be easy to keep—you just keep silent. However, if you're a democratic institution, not only will you need to keep silent, you will eventually be put in a position of having to lie to or misinform the public.

What the military and government don't appreciate is that when the truth about the extraterrestrial presence comes out, a lot of people are going to be very upset. I personally think far more people will be enraged at the lies and coverups than will be distressed about the fact that the aliens actually exist.

The majority of people researching this subject have been frustrated by the indignation of authorities. There is often a feeling that those who have contributed to building our society are entitled to know. Most people are responsible enough to know. For crying out loud, there are problems in the world that are much more serious and frightening than the extraterrestrial presence!

The Future of the Military

In the kind of world that we'll need to evolve into if we're to survive as a species, there won't be much room for the military in its current form. We will have to find a way to resolve conflict without resorting to violence.

How we'll get there, I don't know. The paradigm shift in human thinking will have to be so profound that I have no idea what the final result will look like. I only know that it has to happen if we're to survive. And however it happens, I don't think the military has much of a future. For this and other reasons, I don't think it will be productive to try and engage the military at this point. For progress in this issue, we need to engage our elected politicians, the ones who actually develop and influence social policy.

How Do We Engage Governments?

*"Evidence shows that public panic is rare and most
rare when people have been candidly informed!"*
—Dr. Vincent T. Covello, founder and director of the Center of Risk Communication

Governments must be made aware that public panic is very unlikely and most unlikely when people have been candidly informed. If this misunderstanding could be addressed effectively it would encourage governments to engage those who are researching this phenomenon. It will be important for governments to understand that when large numbers of people see UFOs or experience contact they may have no framework for understanding or assimilating their experiences. We exist in a social environment in which people talking about UFOs or contact are thought to be crazy. Understandably, such people are going to feel separate, apart, and alienated from society.

During a seminar question period a lady asked me why we should engage governments in the UFO solution. I responded with the idea that almost all governments are notorious for making bad decisions when faced with a crisis they are not prepared for. More and more people are observing UFOs and experiencing direct contact. The phenomenon is also changing and is showing itself more frequently and over more populated areas. At some point, the government will need to acknowledge this reality and begin developing polices and putting resources together to deal with it. It would be in everyone's best interest to provide advice to the government on this subject in the hope that the policies, strategies, and resources are appropriate.

Approaching Politicians

*"Who knows where it came from? A lot of people saw it,
and I saw it too. I would now like to set the record
straight, my office did make inquiries as to the origin of
the craft, but to this day they remain unanswered."*
—John Fife Symington III, former governor of Arizona

On March 13, 1997, a massive extraterrestrial craft was seen by thousands of people in Arizona, primarily the Phoenix area. Hundreds of calls flooded the office of the governor of Arizona. His response was to downplay the events by a public display that could only be described as desperate. His job was to stem the panic and he believed his only option was to make fun of anyone who thought it was a UFO. He later regretted how he responded to it but confessed he was given no support from any other government officials. In fact, he acknowledged that he had also seen the object on the night in question and knew it was extraterrestrial in origin.

I'll actually feel a certain amount of sympathy for the government officials in power when this issue comes to a head. Their constituents are going to be venting a huge sense of betrayal and outrage, and the current government will be the target. But the poor elected representatives will be protesting that it all happened before they came into power, and they don't know what's going on. They will claim that they were not briefed and that they had no help from other government departments. There will likely be a mad scramble to find someone, *anyone*, who might offer guidance to these officials. The former governor of Arizona is now trying to help others not repeat the same mistakes he made. He knows that many officials are going to require a better understanding of how to respond to the public when such events occur.

From a social-management standpoint, the extraterrestrial issue could be far more difficult than global warming and have far deeper ramifications. This is why we need to invite politicians to the table and make them aware of the reality of the situation *now*. Again, let's draw a parallel with the global warming issue. The evidence for global warming accumulated for some time before the catalytic events occurred and governments started to act. Even now, many politicians don't really grasp the issues involved in global warming, yet they're forming policies! The matter came to a head and society demanded action, so politicians are passing legislation without having the depth of understanding that they need. This is why we need to start the process of educating them about the extraterrestrial phenomenon now, so that when the catalytic event happens, they don't go off half-cocked.

I believe that contactees' organizations and interested individuals should start to think about approaching some of our senior politicians and saying, "Are you aware of this? Would you be willing to hear some ideas regarding what government should be doing?"

Before we do this, though, we'll need to create a "proof package" comprising our strongest combination of witness statements, video footage, and physical evidence. Governments spend other peoples' money, so it's not unreasonable to think that they will want some sort of proof before they commit to doing anything that takes money. Once the proof package is assembled, we can start to approach our politicians with some recommendations as to how they might handle what's going to be coming.

What Levels of Government Will Be Involved?

"Of course it is possible that UFOs really do contain aliens as many people believe, and the government is hushing it up."
—Stephen William Hawking, Lucasian Professor of Mathematics, University of Cambridge

Although the conceptual direction and funding for major

initiatives like a coordinated reporting agency may come from the federal level of government, front-line disaster planning and crisis response have historically been the responsibility of municipalities. In most countries, municipalities are responsible for local disaster planning within their boundaries. The logistical aspects of pandemic planning, for example, are all carried out at a municipal level. The broad strokes are initiated at the federal level, but the details are all carried out at the municipal level.

In my opinion, the most productive administrative structure for government action regarding the contact phenomenon will be to have a federally regulated organization provide funding, with the provinces and states determining how that money is spent and how the various issues are handled. The bulk of government involvement in the contact process should definitely come at the municipal level. One reason for this is that the moment you deal with emergency response issues on a federal level, you're likely dealing with the military. To me, it makes more sense that the issues be dealt with mostly at the smaller levels of government and that the military not be involved. The only thing we really need from the military is its commitment not to interfere. There would have to be some way that the military could make its concerns known if it felt that national security was truly being threatened, but other than that, I don't think the military should have a role in how this is handled.

Based on my experiences in municipal service delivery, I'm predicting that the response from municipal, provincial, and state governments will be far more productive than any response from the federal level. In my experience, the smaller, more regional levels of government are much more open to investigating the contact phenomenon and deciding how to respond.

Not only is small government easier to approach, it's also far more human. Big government can be very impersonal; by contrast, municipal governments are likely to be in much closer contact with their constituents and to deal with them on a more human level. This makes it far easier for individuals to approach government and influence its actions.

It's vital that we commit to a constructive approach in all dealings with government. Providing friendly information and assistance will always accomplish more than taking an adversarial position. We need to keep local governments well-informed and make sure that they in turn keep their constituents informed as to how the information is being gathered and shared.

What Should We Be Asking Governments to Do?

"Evidence shows that the longer officials withhold worrisome information, the more frightening the information will seem when it is revealed, especially when it is revealed by an outside source."
—Outbreak Communication Guidelines, 2005 World Health Organization

Ideally, governments will respond to this challenge in the same manner they use to respond to any potentially destabilizing event: collect data, evaluate the situation, and develop an evidence-based response plan. Governments should view this situation in much the same way that they view pandemic planning, by providing resources for assessment, monitoring, and response.

It is inevitable that governments will have to address this issue and numerous reasons why they should do it now. But where do we start? The first problem will seem pretty obvious. How do you get people to trust a government that has chosen to ignore this issue and even ridiculed people who have been attempting to educate the public about its reality? To get people to trust the government on this issue is going to be a tall challenge but not insurmountable. There are five main issues governments have to consider.

1. TRUST

The greatest challenge with informing the public about the UFO phenomenon will be the issues surrounding trust. The government will need to restore some level of trust with the public. Polls indicate that over 50 percent of people in North America already believe that UFOs are real, which means that a significant part of the population has already decided not to trust the government. On issues surrounding UFOs, when the government decides to provide more accurate information, it will have to be done in a manner that would help restore some level of trust.

2. TRANSPARENCY

To continue to build public trust the government will have to put systems in place that guarantee total candor. Credible UFO researchers will be asked to play a much different role, as they will now be perceived as having a record of honesty and dedication to seeking and reporting on the truth. Those who had been considered by many to be fringe scientists as UFO researchers will have to play a much larger role in the future in communicating new government initiatives and scientific findings to the public.

For those claiming sightings, encounters, and abductions, the rights of individuals must be respected. It's imperative to balance the rights of individuals against the information directly pertinent to the public good and the desire for reliable information. The release of government files on UFOs by some countries is a good step in the right direction. It suggests a desire for greater transparency on the subject with the public.

When limits to transparency become excuses for unnecessary secretiveness, the likely result will be a loss of public trust.

3. UFOS ARE REAL

Announcing that the UFO phenomenon is real must be carefully planned. The timing, candor, and comprehensiveness of the message of messages will make it the most important of all communications regarding the UFO phenomenon. It will set the tone for how the government will respond to it.

We know that eventually it will be fully revealed from internal sources or external sources. Major indisputable sightings and a country such as China announcing definitive proof are just some possibilities. So it makes sense that to reduce rumors and misinformation and to frame a single or multiple UFO events, it would be best to announce that UFOs exist and do so as early as possible.

Do we have to worry about how people will respond? Of course we do. We already know from research that people are far more likely to overestimate the risk when information is withheld. Therefore the benefits of announcing that UFOs exist right now outweigh all other risks. Even the risk of providing inaccurate information can be minimized with the appropriate communication message.

4. PUBLIC

The UFO communication messages prepared for the public must include information about what the public can do. People are entitled to information that affects their lives and their families. Therefore communicating with people about specific measures or activities they can take is very useful because it empowers them to take action. Not only do they feel less helpless, but there will be a clear picture of what contributions they might be able to make to help all of us understand what is happening.

5. PLANNING

It is well known that decisions and actions of officials have more effect on trust and public risk perception than communication. To clearly communicate the level of risk to the public it will be important to integrate the message with risk analysis and risk management. Risk communication should be incorporated into preparedness planning for major UFO events or announcements.

I don't mean to suggest that communications regarding UFOs or extraterrestrials that have not been planned for are doomed to failure. It just means a little bit of planning would go a long way to ensure there is an appropriate response to the phenomenon.

The Change Process

Another way to consider what we must do is to consider the number of changes that will have to happen and how we can manage such changes. There are two types of change: *unplanned* change and *planned* change. From our perspective, the aliens' actions are creating an unplanned change for us. The key to dealing with unplanned change is to immediately minimize any negative consequences and maximize any possible benefits. This can be done via planned change, which involves deploying one or more "change agents" to help identify desired outcomes and implement the necessary actions to reach them. To respond to the emerging situation, governments should start considering implementing a planned change.

In order to be effective, any planned change must follow this three-phase process, first described by Kurt Lewin, a pioneer of change theory:

1. UNFREEZE

Induce a desire in people to change their ideas on the UFO subject so we can minimize their resistance to learning about it.

2. CHANGE

In accordance with this objective, deploy people and technology to the problem, evaluate the results, and modify actions as needed.

3. REFREEZE

Once the desired change is achieved, reinforce outcomes and provide maintenance resources.

Choosing the right type of change strategy is crucial. Possible choices are:

A) FORCE/COERCION

The change agent acts unilaterally from a position of relative power.

B) RATIONAL PERSUASION

The change agent brings about change via persuasion based on knowledge and rational argument.

C) SHARED POWER

This method of change focuses on the building of shared values, group norms, and shared goals. Others are invited to participate in planning and implementing change.

When choosing a change strategy for dealing with the contact phenomenon, governments can eliminate Alternative A. The aliens are here because humanity already relies far too heavily on the force/coercion method of initiating change. Governments must proceed via a combination of rational persuasion and shared power.

Since both these strategies allow citizens to exercise their free will, it becomes critical to be able to create a *desire* for change. Before we can create desire, it's helpful to know why change might be resisted. The basic sources of resistance to change, and some ideas on dealing with them in this situation, are:

1. FEAR OF THE UNKNOWN

We must inform people about the nature and purpose of the intervention and outline its potential benefits.

Government may have its own fears, and these must be alleviated but not trivialized. We need to correct any misinformation the government may have been given regarding the likelihood of panic. A 1947 Gallup poll showed that 90 percent of respondents thought that UFOs were not real. By contrast, a 2002 opinion poll conducted by the CIRM Institute, an Italian research firm, showed that 55 percent of respondents believe there is a foundation of truth for the existence of UFOs. In some countries, the vast majority of people believe that extraterrestrials are real and are visiting us. If governments are properly advised and take deliberate action, there will be no panic.

2. NEED FOR SECURITY

We must be honest with the public about the risks of this interaction and provide some means for people to feel safer or to contact an organization they can trust when they need help or advice.

3. NO FELT NEED TO CHANGE

Some people will feel there may be no need to change how we have been dealing with the phenomenon. People should be made aware of how the phenomenon is changing and some of the problems it's creating, and their opportunity to participate in a solution.

4. VESTED INTERESTS THREATENED

The classic solution for this situation is to enlist key people or interest groups in change planning. However, some groups with vested interests, such as the military, scientists, NASA, religious leaders, and UFO organizations, may throw up active roadblocks or be unwilling to participate in specific initiatives by the government. This must be acknowledged and planned for.

5. CONTRASTING INTERPRETATIONS

Some people may be convinced that aggressive resistance to the alien presence is a more prudent course of action, while others would disagree. Still others will assume extremist viewpoints based on poor or misleading information. To address this, those responsible for changing our approach to the UFO phenomenon must provide valid scientific information and facilitate its dissemination to the public.

6. POOR TIMING

The classic solution for this situation is to wait for a better time to inform the public. It's difficult to argue that there will be a better time than now. So I submit that we must act immediately.

7. LACK OF RESOURCES

The government will need to provide supporting resources and also perhaps mobilize a volunteer sector that can supply additional resources.

Research and experience have shown that in order for planned change to be successful, it must follow a specific implementation paradigm:

1. clarify purpose and objectives

2. establish basic operating principles; clarify and communicate shared values

3. develop strategies, policies, and procedures

4. delineate the tasks required to implement change

5. ensure adequate facilities and equipment

6. acquire and train personnel to execute tasks

7. implement the change initiatives

8. monitor the results, and adjust the plan as needed

Key comments regarding some of these steps are made in the sections that follow.

Purpose and Objectives

The purpose of the initiative will be to gather and analyze information on the contact phenomenon, to formulate policies and actions based on the data analysis, and to provide support services to all people who may observe UFO activity or have direct contact with their occupants.

Strategies, Policies, and Procedures

The ethical ramifications of any data-gathering activities will need to be addressed. In particular, people reporting should have their confidentiality and safety guaranteed, as well as freedom from mandatory medical or psychological treatment. It must be very clear that the point of the initiative is to assist all people in dealing with the phenomenon, not to further some hidden agenda of the military.

Tasks Required to Implement Change

DATA COLLECTION

Once we get the government to acknowledge the presence of the extraterrestrials it will be important ask governments to conduct detailed scientific research. We need countrywide reporting systems, ideally coordinated among countries, for people to report sightings and contacts. Within strict privacy guidelines, the information would then be made freely available to the public.

Some countries have already taken steps in this direction. In 1992, Spain's Ministry of Defense opened its UFO sighting files to the public. In the spring of 2007, GEIPAN (Groupe d'Etude et d'Information sur les Phénomènes Aérospatiaux Non identifiés), a unit of CNES, the French space agency, launched a website making its UFO sighting data available to the public. The site will eventually contain all eyewitness UFO reports reaching back to 1954, when record-keeping started. These are fine examples of the government accountability that we should all be striving for. Film footage, pictures, and the results of any investigations should all be freely available to the public via government websites.

In North America, I'd recommend that the agencies responsible for data gathering and dissemination be run by boards of directors composed of nongovernment people who represent key segments of society and key expert groups. The agencies would be government-funded, but the board would report to the public, not directly to government. I think this is necessary for public confidence.

One role of government will be to interface with the military in countries that have advanced detection capabilities, to try and obtain access to some of the military's information. The military may be reluctant to share information because of security concerns. Requests from government will carry more weight than requests from isolated civilians.

As the reporting centers are being developed, we will need to plan how to collect and report the information on sightings so that the developing body of evidence is of maximum value. How will we deal with the reports of actual encounters that people are having? Empathetic as we need to be, it's important to understand that not all people who report experiences or sightings are going to be genuine, or mentally healthy. We'll need to develop clinical diagnostics. What will the process and criteria be for deciding whether a person is telling the truth, whether they're lying, or whether they're mentally ill? How will those decisions affect the information-gathering process? It will be important in doubtful cases to offer help, but to track that data independently of more reliable cases. But at what point does prudence become an attempt to manipulate the data? These issues will all need to be worked out.

We may need to look for some physical means of identifying those who have had contact. Subjective ways of determining who has had contact are inherently unreliable, so it would help to be able to develop some physical guidelines, such as an ability to identify implants. It's likely that the final diagnostic protocol will be a cumulative score based on a number of different factors.

One issue of concern is data bias. The possibility always exists that some people will not feel the need to report their experiences. In order to get the most complete data set possible, we need to make people aware that even if they don't feel that they need any help to adjust to their experiences, we'd like to hear from them anyway. It will be productive to pay attention to people who have these experiences and remain emotionally and mentally healthy.

ORGANIZED REVIEW OF EVIDENCE

After a body of evidence is collected, it should be reviewed by an interdisciplinary team of specialists, including psychiatrists, psychologists, physicians, social planners—a very diverse team. One job of the review will be to look for patterns: Is the number of sightings changing over time? Are there broad "classes" of experience; for example, people who have an implant in the chest versus those who have one somewhere else, versus those who appear to have no implant? Looking for patterns will be a key aspect of understanding the phenomenon and how it might be changing.

We'll need to keep in mind that the data may be skewed. For example, if we set up a help line, who will use it? Would it be people who perceive that they need help? It's possible that there will be contactees who do not report because they adjust to their experiences and feel no real need to get help or share what they've experienced. Some of the data that is available now is certainly skewed. For example, the people that John Mack was seeing likely came out of a certain segment of the population that could afford to pay a psychiatrist to listen to their experiences. There are many cultures and countries where people don't have access to Western-style psychiatrists and psychologists. We may be missing the input of people who have integrated their contact experiences in a healthy way, and feel no need to seek help.

One challenge will be to decide how information and conclusions are disseminated. The public has a right to hear the truth, but at the same time, the more information that is given out, the easier it becomes for fakers to corrupt the database. Some balance will need to be struck.

Information-sharing between countries must be a priority. This is a global phenomenon, so we need worldwide data.

At some time during the process, we'll need to develop a working theory about what is going on and our role in it. If we don't, we cannot hope to respond effectively. But if we approach the process with open minds, and a willingness to look at both the science and the perceptual realities of contactees, then any underlying principles governing the contact process should come to the forefront. Using those principles, we can proceed to plan.

Whatever plans are made, they must be flexible, living documents that can be adjusted as new information becomes available, or as the phenomenon unfolds in unforeseen ways. At this point, I cannot see where our inquiries will lead or what the data will suggest. It's possible that the only outcome will be that our commitment to support those having contact will deepen their relationships with the aliens, and that will be the catalyst for positive results. Perhaps our understanding won't come till much later.

CRITICAL-INCIDENT STRESS MANAGEMENT

The trauma that those witnessing extraordinary UFO events experience may equal the traumas of others who experienced natural disasters, industrial accidents, and other crisis situations. In one sense, the contactee's trauma is worse, because he or she is aware that the aliens can choose to reappear at any time.

People have nowhere to turn for help. Progressive societies must not allow this to continue. One of the most beneficial things that governments can do is provide people with immediate assistance in assimilating their experiences. To provide effective assistance, governments must take the following three steps:

1. Recognize the problem, and commit to a program designed to lessen the traumatic impact of the experiences. Program planning will need to involve people in the fields of psychology and psychiatry at a minimum. Ideally, the reporting system already described will also function as a help-line system, so contactees can be offered immediate help if they need it.

Again, the focus must be on social support, not
military or police involvement.

2. Commit to a timely response. People should
be able to receive assistance within twenty-four
hours after an incident, and ideally receive it
immediately upon request. Resource allocation
should be made with this standard in mind.

3. Allocate resources, including personnel to
provide counseling, and training for these
personnel.

Acquiring and Training Personnel

Any psychologists retained to work with contactees must be
willing to approach the subject with open minds. In his book
Passport to the Cosmos, John Mack wrote, "The orientation and
ideology of the investigator, and the questions he or she asks or
does not ask, will determine to some degree what data will be
enabled or allowed to come forth and will affect profoundly the
interpretation of the experiences."

Abductees are not generally disturbed individuals and
are relatively easy to treat. They need to encounter others who
will listen to them and take their accounts seriously. Dr. Mack
reported that many abductees experienced great relief and an
improvement in their mental status when they were allowed to
share their experiences with someone who would listen. Support
groups led by someone with a background in the abduction field
can also be of great benefit.

Peer counseling by other abductees working on a volunteer
basis is also an option. It's possible that contactees who are further along in the assimilation process will be able to help new

contactees to incorporate the experiences into their lives. It would have been so much easier for me if I'd had someone to talk with about what had happened.

The Space Program: Continue or Not?

In 2009 I paid a visit to the Kennedy Space Center. It was a dream of mine to see where human technology strove to reach for the stars. To consider that this was done in the 1960s is still difficult for me to comprehend. Yet in 2005, the US military's space budget was just over $12 billion. NASA's proposed budget for 2008 is over $17.5 billion.

In 2005, Canada contributed about $300 million to its own space program and experienced significant cost increases in projects with international partners. It was predicted that Canada's share of the costs of operating the International Space Station would consume about a third of the Canadian space agency's annual budget.

Governments are going to struggle with pulling in the agencies that have worked so independently from the elected officials in keeping the UFO subject secret. Maybe funding space exploration should be withdrawn if information is not shared with the public. After all, it's our tax dollars that are funding these programs. Surely there are ways to inform people without compromising military secrets!

What Governments Should Not Do

It would be naïve to believe that all governments will respond to the extraterrestrials in a positive way. There may be governments that will respond in a very negative way, for example, with attempts at military force, or by repressing people who are reporting encounters. Will the military view people who speak openly of having had contact as security threats or, even worse, as "collaborators with the enemy?" It's not that far-fetched. Consider the treatment of Falun Gong supporters in China. Some militaries have a history of acting very aggressively against anyone who threatens the status quo. We will need to make sure that people reporting UFO sightings or contacts are protected from such threats.

Similarly, we need to be very careful about making decisions on behalf of contactees. For example, the forced removal of implants should not be allowed. I don't believe that the military or governments should be allowed to remove implants in the name of national security. Each individual should make his or her own decision on this matter.

The mildest form of negative response, of course, would be for a government to remain disengaged and do nothing. To such governments, I simply say:

"Facts do not cease to exist because they are ignored."
—Aldous Huxley

Possible Changes in Social and Government Structure

"It is not the strongest of the species or the most intelligent that survive but the most responsive to change."
—Attributed to Charles Darwin

Our whole system of carving the world up into countries that recklessly compete to dominate one another and the available resources is just not conducive to long-term peace and prosperity.

Our economic systems may need to undergo serious changes too. The current business model, which worships at the altar of economic growth, obviously cannot continue to apply forever. Yet the economic sector carries a great deal of power. Governments trying to move to a low-growth model of sustainability may face severe pressures.

It's hard to describe what a sustainable world will look like, politically and economically, or how it might come about. We cannot say whether it will be a more authoritarian structure, or a totally non-hierarchical structure in which, somehow, no one makes decisions for anyone else. True spiritual awareness could make a huge difference in the way that political and economic decisions are made—but what does spiritual awareness mean here? What's the practical application on a day-to-day basis? These are profound questions. The answers will have to be found.

Our governments can help us down the path of understanding. We have the resources to contend with this phenomenon. We have the ability to deal with it in a responsible manner. Our governments should be helping us to do that. The most enlightened response would be to establish reporting centers, collect and analyze data, report that data to the public, and provide support services for anyone who feels they need help in coping with their experiences.

The current social policy of silence is unacceptable, reprehensible, and immoral. Any repression of facts by military and government agencies, based on the notion that such repression is in the best interests of the people, is an old, autocratic way of thinking that needs to stop. The ship will not stop sinking because the passengers are not being told the true situation. Conversely, if we seize this amazing opportunity, there is no telling what we can build.

8

SCIENCE

"A new scientific truth does not triumph by convincing its opponents and making them see the light, but rather because its opponents eventually die, and a new generation grows up that is familiar with it."
—Max Planck, German theoretical physicist who originated quantum theory

The goal of this chapter is not to attempt scientific explanations of how UFOs and the aliens do what they've been reported to do. Others far more qualified than I, including retired NASA aeronautics specialist Dr. Paul R. Hill (see appendix A), have tackled that question. The goal of this chapter is to start mapping out a basic strategy for the organized scientific study of this phenomenon.

Weight-of-Evidence Principle

The scientific principle of weight of evidence dictates that if the amount of evidence supporting one theory outweighs other competing theories then that one theory is most likely correct.

Why Science Has Turned Away

*"Most ignorance is evincible ignorance. We don't
know because we don't want to know."*
—Aldous Huxley

To date, the silence of the scientific world has been astonishing. Pretend, if you will, that we're all on a spaceship voyaging through space hundreds of years in the future. If the events that have been reported on Earth had ever been reported on that ship, there would be a massive scientific effort to find out what the heck was going on! The best scientists would be involved. Time and resources would be allocated. But here on Earth, the majority of our scientists sit in virtual silence and denial. Why?

There aren't any good reasons—only excuses. How many scientists calling themselves UFO researchers have actually concluded there is nothing to UFOs? None that I'm aware of. The truth is many scientists are constrained by what their peers think of them. There is a long history of revolutionary ideas and truths being violently opposed by the traditional scientific community.

They would do better to start looking for answers. Human reality and human understanding of what is possible are constantly evolving. A thousand years ago, anyone who possessed a cellphone, TV, or motorcar would have been burned at the stake. It would be a dull world if we had learned all there is to know; in fact, I can think of nothing more appealing to a true scientist than the opportunity to study something that's truly mysterious.

At this point, though, science has few answers. As do I. I don't know how, during one encounter, the aliens moved me through a solid wall. I only know they did it. By aligning the atoms in some new kind of energy state? Maybe by access of an alternate dimension that physics has already calculated should exist. Science is going to struggle with these phenomena, because the aliens' technologies and abilities simply surpass our know-ledge of the laws of our physical world.

If my theories about the contact phenomenon are right, the changes that are coming will make global warming look like a tea party. Forget about changing shorelines and beachfront property, this has to do with the survival of humanity, possibly over the next thirty years. To think that our scientific institutions have put so little effort into trying to understand this phenomenon is nearly incomprehensible. There is little doubt that some of these institutions will be shaken to their core. On the one hand, I can't help but cheer at the thought they will collapse. In a more charitable mood, though, I realize that science does not exist in isolation. There are still very good people in science. However, scientific funding is intimately tied to educational institutions, business, technology, politics, and the military, which means that in many cases there are people driving the scientific agenda who may not be pursuing the best interests of the planet, or of human-ity as a whole.

Fermi Paradox Solved

In 1950, four highly distinguished Los Alamos scientists— Enrico Fermi, Edward Teller, Emil Konospinski, and Herbert York—spent time discussing a question posed by Fermi: "If there are extraterrestrials, where are they?"

Fermi's thesis was that if extraterrestrials more advanced than us actually exist, they should have shown up by now. Given that there are plenty of stars much older than the sun, and that at least some of these stars must be orbited by planets, then any developed civilizations that exist in other solar systems should have had ample time to explore the galaxy and reach Earth. The four scientists concluded that even if a relatively slow means of space travel were used, there is no fundamental scientific reason why a technically advanced civilization could not visit vast numbers of worlds. After all, a time span of 100 million years represents only 1 percent of the age of our galaxy! Fermi's deceptively simple question gave many scientists something to ponder. It also challenged the idea that the distances between the stars were too great for an advanced civilization to travel.

Many claim that no one has been able to give a satisfactory answer to Fermi's question, which has become known as Fermi's Paradox. The answer, of course, is simple: the extraterrestrials *are* here, and have been for some time. Mainstream science has simply chosen to ignore the mountain of evidence that points to that fact. Fermi's Paradox isn't a scientific paradox at all. It's a scientific absurdity—the absurdity of assuming that there is no evidence.

Requirements for Effective Scientific Investigation

"The possibility of reduced-time interstellar travel, either by advanced extraterrestrial civilizations at present or ourselves in the future, is not fundamentally constrained by physical principles."
—Dr. Harold Puthoff, director, Institute for Advanced Studies at Austin, author of *Fundamentals of Quantum Electronics*

A primary characteristic of the true scientific investigator is *lack of bias*. If it weren't so tragic, it would be amusing that so many parties claiming to investigate the UFO phenomenon are unable to accept the hypothesis that "it is possible (however unlikely) for an advanced life-form to have evolved outside of our world and to be in contact with human beings at the present time." Refusal to accept even the possibility of an extraterrestrial presence moves an individual from the category of investigator to the category of debunker. True scientific inquiry may start with a positive or negative hypothesis, but it certainly does not make up its mind before the inquiry has started.

For example, when John Mack began his psychological investigation of contactees' reports, his initial assumption was that the cause was some kind of delusional psychosis. However, he kept an open mind, applied all his years of clinical training to *what he actually saw, not what he wished to see or expected to see,* and at the end of his study, concluded that no clinical psychosis could be found, and that the events were being reported accurately and reliably by the majority of these individuals. His conclusions astounded him.

Interestingly enough, when Mack (a Pulitzer Prize-winning author and founder of the psychiatric department of Cambridge Hospital) was accused of using faulty methodology in his study, his response was that he had applied exactly the same procedures and criteria that the psychiatric profession uses in assessing individuals for any other purpose. Based on the standard methodology of his profession, the evidence said that contactees' experiences were real.

The crucial point here is that Mack began from a point of skepticism, not a point of denial. Although doubtful, he proceeded in the true scientific spirit—with an open mind—and therefore made an evidence-based conclusion that was different from his initial opinion. The contactees he worked with were fortunate that he had a truly scientific mind. Had it been otherwise, he could have traumatized a lot of very vulnerable people.

Scientific history is full of obstructionism by researchers and social/political institutions who "know" a particular premise cannot be true. One very timely example involves global warming. Although scientists agree that global warming is occurring, it is not yet clear how much of this warming is caused by human activity and how much by natural cycles. Yet at the present time, scientists who assert that natural events such as volcanic eruptions and solar cycles may be far greater generators of CO_2 than human activity are being subjected to the harshest forms of attack. In some cases, proenvironmental groups have even argued that such scientists should be tried for "crimes against humanity"!

In the truly scientific mind, lack of bias triumphs over all social and political motivations. As far as the UFO phenomenon goes, being unbiased does not mean that the researcher must uncritically accept every tale or piece of evidence that is advanced in support of an extraterrestrial presence. It does mean that the investigator must pursue all possibilities with a fearlessly open mind and dedication to the principles of sound research.

What Has Been Done?

"All truth passes through three stages:

First, it is ridiculed

Second, it is violently opposed

Third, it is accepted as self-evident."
—Arthur Schopenhauer

Within the scientific community, the psychological aspects of contact have been studied more than the purely physical aspects. (Unfortunately, some in the scientific community do not consider psychology to be a science. I personally think they're wrong; we can do experiments, derive repeatable results with large populations, and identify and treat chemical imbalances, all using sound principles of scientific investigation.)

There have, however, been isolated studies of the physical aspects of contact, some made by accredited scientists. When John Mack was placed under review by Harvard University, Dr. Bruce Cornet, a highly qualified geologist and paleobotanist, came to Mack's defense in a letter to the University Review Board, which read, in part:

> Through my own personal experiences I have observed and witnessed this phenomenon, and interacted with this intelligence. From direct field investigation I have overwhelming photographic and geophysical evidence for the existence of these technologies and this intelligence, and for the ability of this species to conceal its activities through the use of technology-assisted mind control techniques and telepathy. My success in obtaining these unprecedented data appears to have been deliberately planned by the nonhumans as part of a long-term agenda to gradually educate mankind without causing undue harm or damage to his religious and socio-economic structures and institutions. I can state from personal contact with this species that their behavior, culture, and appearance are so different from ours that no simple and direct contact is currently possible without overloading man's capability to recover from the intellectual and cultural shock. . . . They want us to know them without fearing them.

Dr. Cornet further wrote:

> I have photographically recorded with time exposures (sometimes with accompanying dynamic

camcorder records) over one hundred night sightings and close encounters, including low fly-overs and spectacular maneuvers of plasma lights in the sky. The shapes of these craft were anything but conventional, and they certainly were not figments of my imagination (there were sometimes multiple witnesses). Their stealth technology is awesome, and beyond anything our military has admitted to having. . . . I have accumulated an extraordinary body of evidence that strongly supports if not proves the existence of intelligently controlled non-human technology on earth.

When detailed scientific observation by a trained professional with a distinguished scientific career produces solid evidence that a thing exists, does it make any sort of objective sense to argue that it "cannot"?

Thoughts on the Scientific Method

"Science without religion is lame, religion without science is blind."
—Albert Einstein

The structure of the scientific community doesn't lend itself to mavericks. Will we ever see another Einstein come out of the scientific community? Probably not, at least not the way the scientific community is currently structured. He'd never make it.

With respect to the UFO phenomenon, the scientific community is caught up in a Catch-22 of denial:

Why aren't you investigating this?
There is no solid evidence about UFOs.

Have you looked at all the available evidence?

No, because the distance between worlds is too great.

What about [insert any piece of available evidence here . . .]

That cannot be considered good evidence because it doesn't coincide with my first assumption that UFOs couldn't be here because the distances between the worlds is too great.

It's ridiculous to make a proclamation that there is no scientific evidence to support the conclusion of an extraterrestrial presence. Some may refer to the lack of repeatable laboratory testing. There are many things in science that don't just happen in a lab. They happen in the real world and for those situations we must use direct and indirect observations. The investigator or observer has no control over all the variables. In my years of work with accident/incident investigations, the collection of information and evaluation of evidence after the incident has occurred are based on strict scientific principles. I have learned the importance of avoiding formulating conclusions until all the evidence has been collected and impartially studied. Evidence includes testimony, written and verbal statements, collaborating testimony, videos, photos, disturbed ground, radar, memos, etc. These are all completely legitimate modes of scientific investigation.

Some scientists have publicly stated that unless a UFO lands in their backyard and they get to meet the extraterrestrials personally, they won't believe that extraterrestrials exist. To state that personal evidence is the only kind you'll accept is certainly not good science. Do these people ever read scientific journals? If so, do they refuse to accept results obtained by others, simply because they themselves have no personal experience of the result? Of course not.

There is a very odd distortion taking place in the area of UFO research. In any other field of study, evidence collected by a scientist of repute would be viewed as proof in support of the thesis being investigated. Yet in the UFO field, when respected scientists investigate, the chief response of the scientific community seems to be to try to shift that person from the status of respected scientist to that of "fringe element crank who has lost objectivity." Throughout history, science has progressed by investigating observed phenomena that were not fully explainable within the framework of current understanding. Why should such an approach suddenly be deemed unscientific, or be grounds for disparaging an individual's scientific competence?

It's true that some UFO researchers may become passionately and personally involved in their work. Many great minds, when in search of truth, become personally involved. Yet in the field of UFO investigation, personal involvement is seen as the kiss of death, yet another reason why the investigator has lost objectivity. What nonsense! No one would dare tell a cancer researcher who had entered the field after losing a relative to cancer that he or she had lost objectivity. Personal experiences that provide insight into the nature of the UFO phenomenon are not to be rejected; such personal experience is extremely valuable to any investigator in any field of study.

We must ask *why* the scientific community seems determined to cast aspersions on anyone involved in UFO research. It seems that some are so threatened that they need to discredit anyone who might tell us the truth.

Possible Areas of Investigation

Investigating UFOs will be very difficult for scientists who are used to thinking in narrow terms of laboratory scientific methods. They seem only to be willing to study things in which they can control all the variables. In this situation, it's very difficult to formulate a theory, execute a well-designed experiment, then collect and analyze evidence. This assumes that the evidence is readily available. The possibility of capturing one or more aliens and subjecting them to controlled experiments seems nonexistent. I am not suggesting that we attempt to do such a thing.

We therefore need to acknowledge the strength of other commonly used scientific methods of investigation and concentrate on working with the evidence that we have and are able to collect. The interpretation of that evidence may be the most difficult and frustrating aspect of this work. Some scientists are already forced to work this way. Astronomers, for example, don't have the ability to blow up distant stars just to see what happens. Essentially, they sit around and wait until nature obliges them, then collect a broad spectrum of data and analyze it to see if anything useful turns up. At least for the present, this is the approach that UFO researchers will need to take. Eventually, from observation and data sharing, understanding should follow.

Within UFO research, there are two basic areas of investigation: psychological investigation and physical investigation. These are described below.

Psychology

Because the aliens are contacting individuals, much of our scientific investigation will necessarily involve the psychology and subjective experiences of individual contactees. It will be important to work with large numbers of contactees, so that overall similarities and trends can be identified. Once that is done, the resulting profile can become a diagnostic tool for evaluating whether or not any individual has likely had contact. The potential pitfall, of course, is that fakers can use the profile information to corrupt the data set by reporting false experiences. (How ironic that the scientific method demands repeatability, yet as soon as you use repeatability as a diagnostic criterion, you open up the opportunities for charlatans.) The best way to minimize the possibility of fraudulent reporting would be to find a way to physically measure who has had contact. Opportunities for developing physical diagnostics are discussed later in this chapter.

One role of psychological investigation will be to build on John Mack's work to try to pinpoint the kinds of psychological changes that occur in contactees over time. It will also be important to see if the basic psychological nature of the experience is changing or evolving in any way.

In assessing any set of data, it will be important to remember that the data may be skewed. For example, studies made by a private psychologist or psychiatrist (such as John Mack) may be skewed in favor of contactees who could afford such treatment. Even with data obtained from a funded agency, it's important to remember that not all contactees will choose to report.

A bigger problem for science, however, is that the abduction phenomenon is intimately involved with human consciousness, and any real understanding of consciousness is still on the outskirts of traditional science. One reason for this is that it's virtually impossible to talk about consciousness without talking about spirituality. Once you become truly conscious of your environment and your true relationship to it, how can you separate that knowledge from spirituality, which is the drive to maintain all the elements in balance in an interrelated system?

We've tried very hard to separate religion and spirituality from science. The two had their battle, and here in the Western world there was an agreement that each would go off and do its own thing. So it will be difficult for science to enter areas that are ultimately involved with the questions of human spirituality and the overall prosperity of the planet. However, that's where we'll eventually have to go if we want to continue as a species.

Physical Evidence

Although much of our investigative work will focus on human psychology, it's still important to continue to try to establish clear physical evidence to corroborate abductees' reports. We already have physical evidence that craft have left behind when they have landed.

Physical evidence is desirable because it provides a very objective way of measuring certain parameters. As such, it has the potential to relieve abductees of the burden of persuading themselves and others that the bizarre events they have undergone are truly real. Physical evidence will help society and government to accept the reality of the phenomenon, and once reporting centers are established, physical evidence will help to validate the reports of people coming forward to report encounters. Physical evidence may also be of value in categorizing different types of abduction experiences, thereby helping us to understand the phenomenon.

SCARS, CUTS, ETC.

There are a number of reasons that we may not be able to assign a high degree of importance to physical evidence such as scars, cuts, scoop marks, and bleeding noses. One problem is that there is no real consistency between the size, location, or type of marks or scars reported by different abductees. Another problem is that all these physical characteristics can have very mundane explanations. For example, bleeding noses can occur from a variety of medical and environmental conditions.

These kinds of marks may well result from an abduction experience, but they're not definitive evidence. Conversely, not having such marks does not mean that a contactee is lying. In 1987, a probe was inserted through the left side of my abdomen into my stomach, but I show absolutely no scarring as a result. For these reasons, I'm not confident that this area of focus will provide any important insights.

IMPLANTS

Alien implants are the most challenging, yet the most promising, category of physical evidence available. In and of itself, the presence of a foreign object in a contactee's body means nothing. Certainly you can pull something out of an individual, but what is it? A piece of metal, a piece of rock? Fine—did this person get shot with a BB gun? Did this person have an accident when they were young and get a piece of gravel embedded in their thigh?

It may be difficult to locate implants, and even more difficult to prove that they are of alien origin. X-rays will likely not be useful. When I had a neck X-ray for unrelated reasons, I scrutinized it carefully, but my implant was completely invisible on the X-ray. (This means only that the implant is similar in density to human tissue.)

What features might an implant be expected to have? An alien implant might be composed of material that does not originate on this Earth or that is fabricated using a process unknown to us. It might demonstrate a biomechanical design characteristic not consistent with other known human biological functions. Ideally, it will have a demonstrable, measurable function. For example, if an object were found to be transmitting signals, that would be strong evidence. (I personally think that if the implants are transmitting signals, it will be in some manner that's beyond our detection capabilities.)

Alternatively, the implant might appear as a physical or physiological anomaly with no discernable function, but be found in the same physical location in a significant number of abductees. An object that appears otherwise unremarkable, but is consistently found in the same location in a large number of contactees, may be an implant. There is likely more than one type of implant being used. It may be that the objects have some kind of protein coating to prevent the body from rejecting them, or they may be of a metal substance tolerated by the body. If we found an object that was constructed of material that did not exist on Earth, or demonstrated a physical or physiological anomaly that appeared to have a measurable purpose or function, that would be a good indicator that we truly had found an implant. If we could identify and determine the function of implants, that would be a huge step. However, it's vital that all research on implants be done only with the full consent of the participants.

If a method for detecting implants can be found, it might provide a rapid screening method for potential contactees. It would be a conditional test—in other words, if you have one, you're a contactee, but if you don't, no conclusion can be made.

Whether or not contactees have detectable implants, it might be a good idea to put monitoring equipment on volunteers who have had contact, concentrating particularly on the central nervous system, to look for abnormalities or unusual growth patterns.

We must guard against information abuse. From a scientific point of view, it's completely desirable to quantify this kind of information. However, hard data is a double-edged sword, and the possibility of abuse exists. Do we really want some disturbed person running around killing contactees under the impression that doing so will save the Earth? Taking a broader view, it's always possible (although I think unlikely) that we will find out that the aliens' intentions are not good. What happens to contactees then?

Will they be forced to undergo implant-removal operations? Let's hope we don't have to deal with such issues.

EXTERNAL TRACES OF THE CRAFT

Once our reporting centers are established, we will need to systematically investigate every UFO report to see if there has been physical evidence reported or left behind.

We need to make every effort to study the craft and understand them. Right now, we're caught in a Catch-22: according to our understanding of physics, craft that can travel at 6,000 mph and make sudden right-angle turns do not exist. Therefore, the reasoning goes, these reports must be false. Since they are false, there is no reason to study further. This must change. Just because we don't yet understand something doesn't mean that it's not possible. We need to accept the fact that there may be more to our world than we have yet discovered.

What Science Needs Is . . .

"If an elderly but distinguished scientist says that something is possible he is almost certainly right, but if he says that it is impossible he is very probably wrong."
—Arthur C. Clarke, author of *2001: A Space Odyssey*

What science needs is a good kick in the ass.

Pardon the bluntness, but it's true. Proving the existence of the extraterrestrials will not be that difficult. In fact, it's the easiest part of the whole puzzle because the evidence is already there and it's overwhelming! The real challenge will be to understand what they're doing and decide on our response.

Many feel that the holy grail of science, and our scientists, have let us down. Our organizations have let us down. However, assigning blame is not very constructive. Our politicians and scientists currently operate within a rigid social system that makes it a tangible risk to respond to the emerging phenomenon. Why would they stick their necks out?

What the scientific community needs is a maverick, somebody with courage and credibility who's willing to get into everyone's face and say, "Such and such is happening, and you guys all need to take this seriously. Let's go! Here are the policies that need to be in place. Here's what you have to do."

I believe that the overall evolution of this process will be similar to the evolution of the environmental movement—in that case, expert opinion finally garnered public support, and the government started to act. In the field of extraterrestrial relations, we need a few outspoken experts to initiate the process, and it has to start *now*, not after the crisis comes. Crisis planning that comes after a crisis is seldom effective.

What's at stake is nothing less than human survival. Come on, guys, what could be more exciting to a scientist than discovering something with the potential to change human history?

9

FOR CONTACTEES: ASSIMILATING

"When I tell any truth it is not for the sake of convincing those who do not know it, but for the sake of defending those who do."
—William Blake

Although the contact process may be beneficial to humanity as a whole, it is certainly stressful on individual abductees. These experiences can be emotionally and physically disturbing, incomprehensible, and traumatic, but also exciting and liberating—sometimes at virtually the same time.

Initial encounters are characterized by a sense of confusion and vulnerability, frequently accompanied by a variety of symptoms typically associated with post-traumatic stress. There may also be odd physical manifestations. Abductees may report waking on top of the covers or upside down on the bed, in a room of the house other than their bedroom, or sometimes even outside the house. Their clothing may have been removed. Clothing may be found neatly folded by the bed, or may never be found. Abductees who were driving may find themselves many miles from their last conscious location. They may be much closer to their destination or, in some cases, far off their intended path.

Abductees who do not want to believe their experiences can find such physical manifestations frightening, while others find the physical corroboration helpful in reassuring them of their sanity—something really *did* happen.

No one knows how many people have come to terms with these contact experiences without seeking outside advice or help. At this time, there is no way to measure or collect this information. What's certain is that some people have found the experiences troubling, but have chosen to live in a kind of self-enforced isolation rather than risk the disbelief and ridicule (and perhaps the "crazy" label) that they would likely receive if they were to talk about their experiences.

The number of people seeking therapy for abduction experiences continues to grow. This indicates that increasing numbers of rather ordinary, psychologically healthy people are reporting unusual experiences with strange beings who are not of this world. Whether or not society believes their accounts, these people have been traumatized by what they consider to be very real and frightening experiences that are beyond their control. At present, they have few resources to help them. This chapter is an attempt to discuss some key issues that may benefit contactees who feel a need to search for answers.

Although the goal is to provide some sound practical perspectives, the first rule for anyone trying to assimilate their contact experiences is this: *make up your own mind.* Your relationship with the aliens, and your decisions about its meaning, must develop from your own beliefs and perspectives, not my opinions or the opinions of others. So take what makes sense, and gently leave the rest behind.

Are You a Contactee?

You may have wondered if you're a contactee. There are several experiences that can indicate that contact may have taken place.

Some of them are listed in the table on page 62. Taken individually, each of these experiences can have alternative explanations. However, the more of them that a person has experienced, the more likely it becomes that that person is a contactee.

If you've ever experienced so-called sleep paralysis, during which you've awakened during the night experiencing a suffocating sense of paralysis, accompanied by feelings of extreme dread, you may have had contact. This feeling is found among many contactees. (I myself have experienced this paralysis a number of times throughout my life, but didn't understand what it meant until much later. I once asked a Catholic priest about it, but he could not offer a satisfactory explanation.) Other contactees report feeling as if there were a physical presence in the room; still others report seeing small beings with large eyes. Some contactees exhibit strong feelings of vulnerability, with generalized anxiety. Other common symptoms include insomnia, fear of the dark and of being alone at night, covering windows against intruders, sleeping with the light on (as an adult), and disturbing dreams and nightmares, especially when the dreams are associated with flying craft and alien ships that take the person away. Sounds, smells, images, or activities that the contactee finds disturbing for no apparent reason may later prove to be associated with the abduction experience.

In many cases, the contact process begins very early in life. Contactees often report that, as children, they saw little men or other beings in their bedrooms, or experienced a feeling of a presence. Some have reported close-up sightings of strange objects in the sky during the day or night, or even seeing unexplained or bizarre bright lights in their bedrooms or other rooms in the house. They may also report, in association with UFO sightings or independently, unexplained time lapses of an hour or more, or finding themselves somewhere away from their home with no memory of how they got there. In the period before they realize they are abductees, some people are strangely drawn to the UFO phenomenon while others do not exhibit the slightest interest.

The first conscious contact can be a reality-stopping moment. After my first physical contact, it took all my energy just to try and remain grounded. It felt as if my innocence had been lost, and the building blocks of reality had crumbled under my feet. If you're feeling that way, my first advice is to concentrate on staying grounded. Do normal things. Take up a physical activity, or any activity that requires your total concentration for short periods of time. Even if you don't feel that you can tell your friends, try to do things with them that you used to enjoy. Allow yourself some time to come to terms with what's happened.

Assimilating Your Experiences May Take Time

Somewhere down the road, after you've spent some time digesting your contact experiences, it can be easy to look back, connect the dots of your experiences, and say, "Well, it's obvious now how these different experiences fit together and what I was supposed to learn from them." When you're in the middle of your first experiences, however, this is highly unlikely. While these events are happening, you can tear your hair out trying to see some way to integrate the experiences into your normal life.

Don't be surprised if you feel confused, anxious, frightened, and as restless as if you're sitting in an anthill. To meet the aliens is to have your perceptions of the world altered (some say destroyed) forever. Our society has constructed a consensus about what is real, and when something intrudes into that reality and shreds it to pieces, the result can be devastating. In truth, your reality has expanded, but it's difficult to try and reconcile the new information with your previous understanding, because some of your previous knowledge has turned out to be false. One survey conducted by PEER showed that nearly half the people reporting abduction experiences were profoundly affected by them, because the experiences had challenged their basic beliefs about the nature of reality.

One thing that makes the contact relationship especially difficult is that it's not like a human relationship—you can't just call the aliens up and talk whenever you have questions. In the search for answers, you're pretty much on your own. You can't end the relationship either; whether you like it or not, they control the agenda. You have no idea whether you'll see them tonight, tomorrow, or ever again. Even if you come to understand that they're in your life for a reason, you will often be unsure about where the relationship is leading and how it will benefit you in the long run.

Assimilating your experiences might take time. It took me twenty years to be able to assess my experiences emotionally and intellectually, and convey my understanding of what's going to happen and what effect my experiences have had on me. (Of course, I had more immediate priorities for much of that time: career, marriage, raising a family. As I'll stress later in this chapter, the here-and-now has to take precedence.) So don't be surprised if clarity takes time.

You're Not Losing It, and You're Not Alone

Simplistic as it sounds, it can be a great comfort to know that you're not alone in this. Reading about others' experiences can be reassuring, especially if they have assimilated those experiences and can attest to their long-term benefits. To try and understand my own experiences, I learned as much as possible about the phenomenon through study and personal experience. This type of reaction is not unusual in contactees.

Consider reading one or more of the books listed in appendix A. Those by John E. Mack are especially helpful. Dr. Mack was an exceptionally compassionate man who used well-established investigative methods and standard psychiatric evaluation criteria to show that the contactees he worked with were psychologically healthy people who were telling the truth about their experience and were suffering from post-traumatic stress. (Note: if you plan to undergo hypnotic regression, as discussed later in this chapter, consider postponing any reading about other peoples' experiences until after hypnosis, so you don't subconsciously affect your hypnotic recall process.)

Some people doubt their experiences because they have a dreamlike quality that is unlike normal reality. Contact memories, just like ordinary memories, can be broadly divided into three categories: things you know, things you are reasonably sure you know, and things you aren't sure of. In the first category are major events that fully engage your conscious attention or during which you feel totally present in the moment (for example, being in a car accident, proposing marriage, being abducted while fully conscious). Events in the second category are things that you're reasonably sure happened, for example, to the best of your recollection, you bought gas last Friday. You might hesitate to swear to it in court, but to the best of your recollection, it was Friday. In the third category are dreams, daydreams, and events that took place in highly altered states of consciousness and which you remember only after the fact. Listing your experiences and evaluating the reliability of each one can help you get a handle on the moment.

Don't hesitate to seek help if you need it. If you choose not to tell the people within your life circle about your experiences, it's possible that you may start to develop feelings of separation or alienation. If you sense that you're having difficulty, consider calling a crisis line or other therapeutic agency. Be sure that the person you confide in is able to approach your needs with an open mind. If not, move on quickly. You don't need more traumatizing!

The Internet is a wonderful tool. You may want to try searching for a bona fide contactee's support group and talk to people who will believe you. However, be prepared to run across people who are emotionally troubled. I once met a person over coffee to discuss her experiences, thinking that it would be beneficial for both of us to meet another contactee. It turned out to be a very difficult meeting. It soon became clear to me that this woman was not a contactee and she was suffering from some from of mental illness. My advice would be, when seeking support from others, take the same precautions you'd take for any new social relationship—meet in public the first few times, and maintain your privacy until you're sure of whom you're meeting.

Will Hypnosis Help?

The aliens are quite capable of altering your conscious perceptions. One of the most difficult aspects of assimilating a contact experience can be living with fragmented memories and being certain that there is more, much more, that you are not remembering. Some contactees choose to undergo hypnosis as a way of restoring the missing information.

The decision to undergo hypnotic regression is not an easy one. It took me about two months to decide; I was afraid of what might happen when I remembered. In retrospect, I'm not sorry that I did it, but neither do I feel the need to go back for another regression each time I have an encounter. The main thing I learned from hypnosis was that I already remembered the really important parts of the encounter. Nothing recalled under hypnosis actually deepened my understanding of the event or its meaning.

One reason not to undergo hypnosis is that it might interfere with the aliens' timing. As discussed earlier, the aliens tend to orchestrate the contact experiences, and the memories, to fit each contactee. Now that I understand this, I can put my personal desires aside and say that if I can't remember certain experiences, that's fine. I trust the aliens, and I've come to believe that I will remember everything that they find is useful for me to know. This is not blind trust. I'm as skeptical as anybody, and I frequently find myself thinking *are they manipulating me? Is this a bad thing or a good thing? Are they evil? Are they good?* These thoughts are to be expected; questioning the experiences is healthy. In my deepest soul, though, I know that the aliens have my best interests, and humanity's best interests, at heart. There are times that this whole process feels like a sacrifice, but that comes with the territory. When (if) the aliens decide that it's time for me to consciously remember more, then it will happen, and I'll do my best to assimilate the information.

Your decisions about hypnosis may not be the same as mine, and that's fine. Your relationship with the aliens is different. The advice I'd give you about deciding whether or not to undergo regression is this: know why you're doing it. Really think carefully about why you want to know. Think about how you will handle what you learn. How will it affect your life? Before you proceed, I'd recommend rereading the material on memory and hypnosis at the start of chapter 4, and thinking about the issues involved. Then, if you choose to go ahead, find a qualified hypnotherapist and make sure that he or she is experienced in conducting regression studies in a way that does not lead the subject into false memories.

Be aware that the inherent uncertainty in the hypnotic recall process makes it a poor tool for the early stages of an uncertain investigation. In my opinion, the information obtained under hypnosis is best filed under "things you think you know," rather than under "things you know." It's easy for anyone familiar with abduction phenomena to color their recall and distort what really happened.

Remember, choosing not to know is a valid choice. Choosing to know is a valid choice as well. If you're feeling tormented and confused—especially when no corroborative physical proof is available—and you're doubting your own sanity, then hypnosis might help to set your mind at rest. You are the best judge of whether it's right for you.

It's Okay to Accept That Parts of This Will Be beyond Your Understanding

One of the hardest parts of a relationship with the aliens is knowing and accepting that you will never fully understand what is transpiring. It can be quite difficult to know that there are aspects of your life that you'll never know about, or be in full control of. It can be difficult knowing that somehow you're involved in an urgent struggle for human survival, but will never really understand the details. You'll catch glimpses of a great mystery, but *you will not be privy to full understanding.*

Accept the fact that maybe you shouldn't be privy to it. This can be surprisingly difficult; anyone who has enjoyed their education, particularly at the college or university level, has learned to thirst after knowledge. You may need to accept that, in this case, more knowledge is not necessarily better. More knowledge may not be beneficial to you.

Let me put it this way: If I have a very important board

meeting planned for Monday morning at 8 A.M., and at 3 A.M. that morning, a bunch of extraterrestrials come into my room, whisk me off to a completely alien environment, administer a number of painful medical procedures, and generally frighten the bejesus out of me . . . would having a clear and lucid recollection of the entire experience help me to succeed in my board meeting? Not likely. Similarly, would having a sudden visceral understanding of all the tragedies that may be waiting to wipe out the human race help me to function in my daily life? Of course not. It's likely that I'd be unable to function at all. It is important not to let these experiences consume you. They cannot rule your life.

Pay Attention to What You Do Remember

When you're looking for the meaning behind your experiences, the clues lie in what you have been allowed to remember. Work with that.

Accept the Fact That You May Be Afraid

In the early years of contact, I spent many days hoping with all my heart for an opportunity to meet them again, and the nights praying to all the gods that they wouldn't come. For years (and years and years), there was not a single night that I went to bed without thinking about them coming, and about how I might, or should, respond. It's rather unsettling to know that they can come into your reality at any time. Now there are nights that I go to bed without thinking about them coming, but it took a long time to get to that point.

It's senseless to berate yourself for being afraid. The contact experience is so strange, so overwhelming, that fear is an inevitable by-product of the experience. If it helps any, I believe that the aliens evaluate all potential contactees very carefully. They aren't here to do you irreparable harm. They give you what you need and what they think you're capable of handling. If they have contacted you, they believe that you have the capacity to assimilate the experience in a positive way.

Take Care of Yourself Physically

Some of the physical procedures that take place during contact experiences can be quite stressful. For example, if you have an implant, you may be undergoing convulsive sessions administered without muscle relaxants, which may result in severe muscle soreness. There are times when I wake up after an encounter and feel a lot of residual muscle pain, almost as if somebody had pounded on my back with a two-by-four. Because I've played sports all my life, I know how my body responds to things, and in these cases, the soreness really should not be there. Also, it's not hard to connect the dots: you remember the aliens coming into the room, and afterwards you have unexplained muscle soreness. It's not hard to extrapolate the experience to other times that you've had inexplicable physical symptoms, and conclude that contact was probably involved, even though you don't recall that experience.

The point here is that contact is a physical process that can have strong physical ramifications. For people who know they're having contact, I'd recommend maintaining good physical health and finding ways to reduce physical tension. Meditation, massage therapy, and other stress-reduction techniques can be very helpful. As the tension is being released from your body, you may experience images and feelings associated with a prior abduction experience; just let them release themselves.

Sleep disturbances can be a real problem. Because many abduction experiences occur at night or when the individual is isolated, contactees may start trying to avoid these situations, resulting in the development of sleep problems. There are no easy answers. If sleep issues are affecting your relationships or your employment, consider looking for help. You're carrying a tremendous load. Be kind to yourself.

Be Here Now

Occasionally someone will say, "Jim, I drove by this UFO once and I keep thinking about it and I'd like to talk to somebody and maybe go through hypnotic regression. I'd like to do this, and this, and this."

And I say, "Why?"

Usually the answer is that they just think it would be a good idea and they want to. So I ask them, "What's important in your life right now?" And I tell them: concentrate on that. Maybe focusing on contact issues is not going to help you with your most immediate needs. It's just a distraction. Your real issues are your health, your relationships, your children, your job. That's where your attention ought to be. Don't let the UFO stuff distract you from what's really important in your life.

Your Earthly problems must always take precedence over the encounters. If the contact-related issues start to impinge on life in the here-and-now, then maybe you need to look at both, but the key to assimilating these experiences, in my opinion, is to *be here now*. This is where God put us, and this is where we're supposed to be living.

If you're feeling dissatisfied or restless, try asking yourself what your life *here* needs? Improve your education, improve your relationships, improve your health, work on your spiritual growth—whatever the issues are—but focus on making this life better and don't worry too much about what's going on out there. If increased social activism is part of your growth, then fine—just make sure that the focus is on what *you* can do, not on lecturing someone else about how they ought to behave. Remember that the best way to influence others is by example. Live the spiritual principles you want manifested in the world.

Stay grounded. Love and nurture your children, attend to your work-related demands. Nurture all your relationships and deal with all the multitude of things that make up everyday life. The aliens think that what we do on a daily basis is very important. If you want to honor the relationship with them, spend time dealing with the issues that are presented to you on a daily basis.

Some people have daily challenges that are far more daunting than knowing there are other beings in the universe. And that's a fact. So focus on the here and now.

Accept the Impact on Relationships

Being a contactee affects every aspect of your personal life. For example, how do you tell someone you love and are thinking of marrying that these beings exist and might come into the bedroom at any time? Will that person decide you're nuts and leave you? If they stay, what will happen? Can you guarantee that nothing bad will happen? Of course not. And you're excruciatingly aware that you might be putting someone you love in danger.

These are real questions that you have to wrestle with. At the very least, you have to cope with the fact that the comfort and intimacy you have with your spouse can be invaded at any time. Parents who want a little privacy from their children can simply lock the door. How do you lock out beings who can float through walls?

There's also the problem of what to tell your children. My wife (who has shared some of my experiences) and I decided that we would tell our children when we thought the time was right. It turned out to be after they had finished high school. In retrospect, it seems to have been a good decision, but there are simply no signposts. What does the whole thing mean for your children? Will the beings abduct them as well? If so, would discussing the abductions help them or hurt them? These are the kind of heart-in-your-mouth questions that you have to wrestle with.

Part of the reason we waited to tell our children until they were older was that we couldn't see any benefit in telling them sooner. I could not, at their stage of understanding, explain the contact in any way that would be meaningful to them. At best, they would have a sort of Star-Trekky understanding of the issue. So we chose to wait. When we finally did tell them, we basically said, "What we have to tell you, we don't fully understand, and you don't have to tell your friends, and we're not even asking you to believe it. We just want you to know that from our perspective, this is what is happening."

It was interesting, because their reaction was more or less, "Yeah, okay," and that was that. They knew us to be grounded, practical parents, and they just said "Okay." They asked a few questions, but I was fairly selective in what I told them, simply that the aliens were real, that I didn't know much about them, and that they had been interacting with Mom and me for a long time. I was surprised at how accepting our kids were. I'm very proud of them, not just for their reaction towards us, but for the wonderful people they've grown to become.

Outside my family, I haven't discussed the experiences with

a lot of people. Sometimes the disclosure decisions are tough. When you think about telling someone, you need to think carefully about how the information will affect them, and how it will affect your relationship with them. The key is to decide if there will be mutual benefit or not. For myself, if I can't be reasonably sure that the outcome will be beneficial for both of us, I say nothing. I'm defining "beneficial" here at a fairly deep level. Obviously, if you tell your fiancée and she leaves you, that's not going to feel very beneficial in the short run, or be the outcome you wanted. However, in the long run it would likely be the best thing for both parties.

Consider Reporting Your Experiences

If your government has a reporting center, you may choose to report the experience. If not, there are a few serious UFO-reporting websites that you may wish to contact. An hour or so on the Web will give you a good idea of who's legitimate and who's not.

The more people who come forward to report their experiences, the more likely the contact phenomenon is to receive the proper attention from government and science. However, before you report, be sure that doing so will benefit you as well.

Seek Meaning and Try to Trust the Process

I'm not naïve enough to believe that the intervention process is without its risks. No matter what the ultimate benefits of having contact, there is a price to be paid. This is an intervention, and as with any intervention, there is a certain degree of trauma, particularly during the initial stages. In this case, the trauma is physical, emotional, and psychological. Perhaps I shouldn't say trauma; perhaps "challenges" is a better word. However you label the process, it will test you. It will redefine what you're made of and who you are.

The aliens tend to teach experientially. Rather than telling you, they will *show* you by linking into your consciousness and giving you images or altered-state experiences that cause you to *experience* the message. At times, these experiences can seem overwhelming, because they carry a depth of emotion that we rarely feel in our waking experiences on Earth. Anyone who's ever had an exceptionally powerful dream with emotional aftereffects that lingered after they awoke has had a small glimpse of what's involved.

As extraordinary as these experiences can be (or perhaps because they *are* so extraordinary), there is much we can learn from them once we begin to trust the aliens. I may not like everything about the aliens, and I may not like everything about the experiences, but I can trust the essential nature of the process and know it is all happening for a good reason. The aliens radiate a feeling of overwhelming love, and I tend to trust that.

Just to restate a couple of key points, the aliens don't want to interrupt our daily lives too much. They want an intimate relationship with us, but at the same time, they don't want to interfere with our lives or our important relationships with each other. For the most part, they want us to continue to experience life the way that we're meant to.

Research has shown that focusing on the spiritual, transformational aspects of the experiences can help abductees to integrate them in a positive way. Within the context of here-and-now human life, abductees should be encouraged to explore and understand various aspects of spiritual enlightenment. The transpersonal perspective is very helpful in this; contactees may wish to refer back to the chapter on Spirituality for more information.

To summarize, don't be surprised if you have mixed emotions about your contact experiences and struggle to understand their meaning. After twenty years, I still have mixed emotions. I've felt terror, wonder, love, frustration, grief, amazement—the whole gamut of human emotion. Slowly, over time, the fear has faded and been replaced with a greater appreciation for the wonder of life. I count myself fortunate to be involved in this small way in one of the most remarkable adventures of human history.

10

WHAT CAN ORDINARY PEOPLE DO?

*"Shattering our limited perceptual view of this reality
will be surprisingly easy. However, the development of
a greater human understanding of our true place in
the Universe will be exceedingly difficult."*
—Jim Moroney

Perhaps you haven't seen a UFO or you haven't, to your knowledge, been contacted, but you want to participate in the evolution of consciousness that humanity is undergoing. What can you do?

What you cannot do, to the best of my knowledge, is choose to be a contactee. It's always possible that at some time in the future, mentally transmitting your willingness might cause you to be contacted, but to the best of my knowledge, it's the aliens who choose who is involved. (Some people who believe in reincarnation have speculated that contactees do in fact choose these contact experiences before being born, but even if that's true, it's too late now. You either chose it before you got here, or it's not going to happen.)

So it's unlikely at this point that humans can initiate contact. We do, however, have the power to make a direct response to this intervention. Both as individuals and as a society, there is one thing we can do to communicate directly with the aliens: accept what is happening.

Our acceptance may mean far more than we think. Although most of Earth's societies have evolved past the point of killing people who think outside of their current norms, we have so far managed to marginalize and ridicule most of the people who have reported contact experiences.

To think that the aliens are unaware of this is naïve.

If we, as a society, wish to be active participants in this intervention, the most important thing we can do is to legitimize what is happening. We must demonstrate to the aliens that we, as a society, are open to what they are offering. What better way to show them than to demarginalize the contact process? If we publicly accept and study the process and support those who witness UFOs or have direct contact with their occupants, we are, in effect, saying to the aliens, "We recognize that you're here. Now what can we build together?"

Legitimizing the contact process does not mean offering uncritical acceptance of every claim or assertion that is made. Legitimizing the contact process means keeping an open mind and searching for answers. It means developing a social climate in which it's not considered bizarre to ask the necessary questions.

Social change is always the product of individual action. The spiritual and social values of many, many individuals combine to form public opinion, which in turn drives government policy, which in turn drives funding for scientific and social outreach programs. For society to change, individuals must take action now. If we're to show the aliens that we are open to what is happening, many, many individuals will need to take action. Here are some possible actions we can take:

State Your Opinions Openly

If we're to succeed in influencing government and social policy, our social frame of reference needs to be shifted at the grass-roots level, so that it becomes okay to sit down over coffee and discuss the UFO phenomenon. If we can't even discuss the topic with each other, how can we possibly expect the government to be comfortable with making proposals to allocate funding for reporting and study? I am not suggesting you support the abduction phenomenon, but at least entertain the idea that there is an extraterrestrial presence here.

Stating your opinion can be surprisingly hard to do. Until now, I've been very selective about whom I discuss the UFO phenomenon with. (Contactees have enough on their plate without adding the possibility of ridicule to the mix.) However, we will all need to be more open about the subject. It's tough to be on the front lines of change, but if we want to avert a catastrophe, that's precisely where many of us will have to place ourselves.

Demand the Truth

We need to say collectively, as a society, that we demand more from our governments. We demand to be told the truth—to be told everything that is known to date about the extraterrestrial presence. We should encourage public hearings into all aspects of the UFO phenomenon.

Encourage Government to Accept the Reality of the Current Intervention

Political and social change often depends on the government's perception of which interest group is the most vocal.

Interest equals votes equals action. It's not possible to help with this intervention by remaining silent; people who don't make their opinions known are not counted by government.

Break away from your fear of ridicule. Start asking questions. Let government know that you take the issue seriously. Voice your opinion, and show your support for organizations or groups that are trying to provide the public with the best possible information about the UFO phenomenon.

It's vital that we engage governments in a friendly way, not by making accusations over past behavior. It's far too late for thinking in terms of blame. The contact phenomenon is evolving quickly, and if my reasoning is correct, we are not far from a breakthrough event. We must provide government with an opportunity to say, "Now is the time," so that our response systems can be put in place without delay. Above all, we need to ensure that government is properly informed, so the policy decisions will be effective and reasonable.

Demand Accountability for Existing Scientific Funding

What are our priorities as a society? Before we decide how to disperse billions of dollars into the netherworld of scientific research, let's think about the value of this research and ensure that the information and results will be disseminated honestly to the public. In particular, demand that the space agency in your country release scientific evidence and information about the extraterrestrial presence. Some portion of any space agency funding must address this issue.

Request Funding for Investigation of UFO Phenomena

One of the best ways to overcome the distortions introduced by fringe groups is to insist that contact research become a mainstream field of science. As discussed in the chapter on government, we'll need to set up a reporting system that is government-funded, but administered by a nongovernment board of directors composed of experts from science, medicine, and the social sciences. Systems for assisting contactees will also need to be set up.

Public education will be a key component. Within the constraints of protecting individual privacy, we must demand that all information that's collected be made freely available to the public.

Ask for Objective News Coverage

We need to encourage the media to report with objectivity. News coverage to date has been a double-edged sword. On the positive side, the media has played a major role in reporting on the UFO phenomenon. Unfortunately, there have been occasions when the subject has been covered in a manner that prevented people from taking it seriously. We can't place all the blame on today's media for that. There is a certain responsibility that we must take in educating the media and providing them with the best information on the subject. If the reporter—no matter how well-meaning he or she is—has been ordered to get *something* on the air by 6 P.M., then they have to take comments from anyone who will speak to them. If reasonable and grounded people are too afraid to speak, then they have to find anyone to speak with. The results can be pretty awful for all concerned.

If we want eyewitnesses to come forth with the courage to tell us the truth, we need to make clear to the media that we want the subject approached in a serious and objective manner. We need to provide the media with the tools they need to make a story worth telling. I have met a lot of good people in the media and they should be commended for their work in getting the truth out.

Support Contactees

We must find ways to help people who are struggling with these experiences. Unfortunately, not everyone making contact reports will be genuine. Some will be fakers, others will be suffering from a mental illness or psychological problem. For this reason, we need to establish reporting centers staffed with people who can assess the validity of each report and direct the person to an appropriate resource, be it trauma counseling for bona fide contactees, or other help for those who are not genuine contactees but who have other issues.

On an individual level, you can support people simply by being willing to discuss the UFO phenomenon and their experiences. If you're open to the information, you may be surprised at what people will tell you. You may never know how much you've helped by speaking three simple words: "I believe you."

Focus on Personal Spiritual Development

Given that human spiritual development is the point of this intervention, each one of us needs to deepen our personal understanding of what spiritual development involves. There's no secret solution for spiritual enlightenment. Different societies and cultures have developed different approaches to the subject. Try to explore a variety of spiritual practices and see how they might contribute to benefitting your life and all life. Examine your own approach to the world: are you part of the solution or part of the problem?

Sustainable Development

Sustainable development will be the future of humanity. We are still missing vital pieces to the puzzle with respect to understanding how our actions directly or indirectly affect our environment. Human beings are a part of the environment and we have the potential to live in harmony with it with minimal impact. We even have the potential to improve and actually enhance this planet's ecosystem. Our world can support vast numbers of human beings, but we will need to have a better sustainable management program in place and it will have to have global implications.

Personal Preparation for Contact

Possibly your prior experiences have led you to believe that the aliens may soon be contacting you. Maybe you think they will never contact you. In any case, each contact is orchestrated specifically for the individual involved; there is really no way to predict how the experience will unfold for you, if it ever does. Therefore it's difficult to give detailed advice on how to prepare. I know reading this book would at least give you a better understanding of what is happening and that should go a long way to helping you cope with it. Another way to prepare may be to learn the basics of meditation and explore other aspects of spiritual development. If you're religious, prayer can be a powerful ally. Even if contact ultimately does not take place, you will have gained something from these preparation activities.

We know that this intervention is becoming more direct, and that it's volatile and dangerous for both species. We know it's been tough on human beings and I am certain the aliens are struggling with it. Their plan of contact appears to be strategic in nature and thus will change and evolve with time. Our best hope is to signal a willingness to proceed.

Since the aliens have initiated the process by showing their craft to groups of people and reaching out to individuals with direct contact, the best way our society can respond is by helping all these individuals to accept what they are experiencing. In this way we are demonstrating a mature-society willingness to understand the human/alien relationship.

11

SUMMARY AND WRAP-UP

"So . . . should we be afraid?"

Someone asked me this question once on a call-in radio program. Unfortunately, it's a simple question that has no easy answer. The aliens aren't here to enslave us or steal our resources. Of that, we need not fear. Yet the future is not going to be easy. The contact process isn't easy, and I wouldn't call anyone a coward if they admitted to feeling fear about what the future may hold. But in spite of the fear, there is so much to be gained.

The abduction phenomenon poses one of the greatest mysteries ever to confront humanity. Someone or something is encouraging an extraordinary evolutionary development in at least a portion of the human population. Within our existing ideas of what is real and possible, it is virtually impossible to find a convincing explanation for what is happening. We cannot account for the fact that thousands of people unacquainted with one another, from small children to grown adults, are experiencing complex, elaborate, and overwhelmingly powerful contact experiences that resemble one another in many characteristic details and are accompanied by a variety of peculiar physical phenomena. Nor can our current understanding of physical reality explain how beings from some other space and time realm can enter our world and affect so many people.

Should we be afraid? I don't think we should be, but if people are afraid, that's certainly understandable. Sometimes I'm still afraid. But we must not be so fearful that we close our minds to the opportunities in front of us. Although we don't know where the aliens are coming from or what kind of world they inhabit, it would be foolish to deny the events they are creating in our world. Whatever is transpiring, our best hope is to meet it with open minds, to try to communicate to the aliens that we want this relationship and we want to know what it is they are trying to tell us.

I believe that the aliens will be seen in our skies much more frequently than in the past. I think that in the future there will be a much more open acknowledgment of their presence, and the amount of contact will increase, perhaps sharply. The phenomenon will continue to grow and evolve. Governments will be forced to respond. There will be an increasing need to help people cope with this frightening and exhilarating new reality. Eventually, our society will demand that we implement some kind of action plan. The paint, brushes, and canvas lie in front of us. What we create now is up to us.

At this point in my life, my conscious contacts with the aliens are few and far between. It seems as if they've decided to let me focus on my own life's challenges for a while, without creating any extra issues for me to cope with. As I've said before, they don't want to overload us. I believe they are aware of our daily lives— the struggles and pains and emotional traumas and challenges and physical ailments that we contend with on a regular basis— and see those things as important. They don't want to upset our lives any more than is absolutely necessary.

Beyond doubt, the experiences have changed me. I'm aware now that there's another reality, one that's much different from the reality that most people know. I'm a gentler person because of the experiences. I have a far greater awareness of the big picture and my place within it. I'm not, by any standard, perfect (nor do I expect to reach that exalted state anytime soon), but I do have a deeper relationship with God, other people, and myself.

Maybe that's all the aliens want for now.

The most exciting thing about the contact phenomenon is that it appears to be occurring worldwide, without reference to race, culture, or class distinctions. The most tragic thing about the phenomenon has been most of humanity's inability to accept that contact really is occurring. The contact experiences can be very difficult. It's unfortunate that some contactees will be hurt because they have to struggle alone within a social vacuum in which there is no psychological support.

The truth is, if we were an intellectually and morally evolved society, the hard scientific evidence and anecdotal evidence that we've accumulated so far would have galvanized a massive amount of interest and led us to allocate significant resources to investigating the contact phenomenon. Except for the billions of dollars allocated to military and space programs, we haven't spent a penny on finding out the truth about alien contact and informing the public. If there has been an outrage involved, it's that we have misdirected our resources towards agencies that are determined to cover up the truth, even if it means ridiculing and isolating those who are brave enough to enlighten the public.

Contact is happening under difficult circumstances, perhaps thousands of years before it should have, but we have run out of time. Our collective actions have put us, and perhaps some other part of the universe, at risk. The intervention is therefore being forced upon us. It's impossible to contemplate all the variables and outcomes that will result from this new relationship.

At some point in time, each human being will have to decide how to respond to the aliens. We will not have the luxury of having our problems solved for us. The aliens are not intergalactic peacekeepers who will take away our nuclear weapons, because the weapons are not the problem. Our willingness—and perceived need—to develop and use the weapons is the problem.

This is a spiritual intervention and we are at the apex of human struggle between good and evil, love and hatred. As nearly as I can express it, the aliens are saying, "You're going to have to evolve as a species. You need to get past the things you're doing to endanger yourselves and all the other life-forms around you. Humanity has a very important role to play in the universe. We're here to correct an imbalance. We're here to help you. We want and need you with us!" The more of us who try to understand this message and give our very best efforts toward change, the more likely it is that humanity will survive and build a new kind of world.

If you were to ask me, "Jim, tell me how all of this is going to happen?" the answer is that I don't know exactly how it's going to happen. I believe that something, some Katrina-like incident or a number of incidents, will trigger massive changes. We will progress in ways that seem impossible at the moment. Before the Soviet Union fell, who would have believed that such a thing would ever happen? Before the Berlin Wall came down, who even thought about such an incredible event? We're facing a new incredible event, one involving the aliens. We may be on the verge of reinventing humanity.

No one will be left unaffected. We're not just looking at a paradigm shift; we're looking at a new reality that will operate in a totally different way. The evolution and direction of humanity will be forever altered and a new chapter will begin. When I was eighteen years old, I had a vivid premonition (appendix B) that something was coming, something of our own doing that humanity would struggle with and barely survive. I think this is part of that premonition. This is humanity's call to arms, and the fight to achieve some understanding is just beginning.

The kinds of changes that we'll need to make to achieve a peaceful, environmentally balanced world will be staggering. Many of us will want to make these changes, but sadly, a significant number of people will be unwilling or unable to do what is needed. Under such circumstances it seems that suffering is inevitable.

The ownership of the world's problems is ours. The responsibility is ours. We have an opportunity to build a new bridge of love and understanding that will extend, not only across our world, but into a new world as well. We owe it to ourselves, to our children, and to all life on this planet to at least try. Whether or not we're afraid, we should be looking at this intervention as a magnificent opportunity. Above all, we need to remember that those who make the best use of any opportunity are those who have prepared for it.

Let's prepare.

"If there is to be a new world, it will be our generation that will have the greatest difficulty living in it!"
—Jim Moroney

APPENDIX A

WEBSITES AND RECOMMENDED READING

http://www.cufos.org/cometa.html—An extensive English-language summary of the French Report "Les Ovni Et La Defense: A Quoi Doit-on Se Préparer?" (English Translation: *UFOs and Defense: What Must We Be Prepared For?*)

http://www.ufoevidence.org/topics/Cometa.htm—The actual text of the above report, available in the form of multiple PDFs.

http://www.bluebookarchive.org/—Project Blue Book Archive. A growing online archive of the US government's Project Blue Book research. Some of the information is government records that have been obtained under the Freedom of Information Act. Volunteers continue to build the online archive of government documents.

http://www.cnes.fr (and *http://www.cnes.fr/web/455-cnes-en.php*)—English and French sites of CNES, the French space agency. The information includes an online database of all UFO sightings recorded by the agency. GEIPAN (a department of CNES) will be putting every eyewitness report since 1988 online. Then, working backward in time, it will add earlier information until all accounts back to 1954 are included. You can search the database by geographic area at: http://www.cnes-geipan.fr/geipan/ recherche.html (the data itself is in French only).

UFOs: The Definitive Casebook, John Spencer, ISBN 978-0-600-57223-7. A compilation of hundreds of sightings worldwide, ranging from sightings later exposed as hoaxes to the many sightings that have never been explained.

Confirmation, Whitley Strieber, ISBN 978-0-312-18557-2. A detailed compendium of proofs. Although I don't always agree with Strieber's analyses, he has compiled proofs from a large number of sources.

Leap of Faith: An Astronaut's Journey into the Unknown, Major Gordon Cooper, ISBN 978-0-06-109877-2. Describes Gordon Cooper's experiences as an astronaut, including his brushes with UFOs. Includes his perspectives on the reactions to UFOs within NASA and the military.

Unconventional Flying Objects, Dr. Paul R. Hill, ISBN 978-1-57174-027-4. A distinguished NASA aeronautic scientist's reports of his UFO sightings, accompanied by extensive research information on how the craft might work.

Paths beyond Ego: The Transpersonal Vision, Roger Walsh, MD, PhD, and Frances Vaughan, PhD, ISBN 978-0-87477-678-2. A clear and comprehensive overview of transpersonal psychology.

Various US government documents: there is a large body of government information that has been released under the Freedom of Information Act. To learn more about what is available and to see copies of these documents, contact:

Fund for UFO Research

Box 227

Mt. Rainier, MD 20712

APPENDIX B

PREMONITION

When I was eighteen years old, long before I knew about the extraterrestrials, I had a premonition so terrifying yet exhilarating, so *real* in its emotional impact, that it has influenced my entire life.

For a couple of days before it happened, I had been feeling a strange uneasiness, as if something really important yet strange was going to transpire. I felt an urge to read up on unexplained phenomena so went to the local library and took out some books to read. A few days later, on a sunny warm afternoon, I began to feel a little tired and thought I would lie down to rest. As I lay on the bed I began drifting out of my body. It was a very peculiar feeling; it felt like something was pulling me. It startled me so much that I leaped off the bed and ran to the door. The experience was deeply unnerving. At first I thought my mind must be playing games on me and it was a result of reading all those darn books. I later recalled that although I read a number of books I was never really satisfied; it was as if I were looking for something but couldn't find it. I stood in the doorway, staring at the large bed, contemplating what was happening and what to do next. There was something definitely happening, but what? I made up my mind I wanted to know. I cautiously returned to the bed, leaned back down, and almost instantly found myself drifting out of my body. Whoo, I thought, I don't recall closing my eyes.

Everything was dark around me. What was going on? I could feel myself continuing to fall or drift, as if I were a ball of consciousness with no physical body. And I was drifting toward something. An image resolved itself—a bridge over a chasm, with a huge wall on the other edge. Then the bridge transformed into a tunnel, and some *thing*, a force of some kind, reached from the other side, grabbed me, and tried to pull me into this tunnel. The force was . . . indescribable. It was alive, a consciousness, and radiating pure hatred and malice that could only be described as evil. Most people with a Christian background might say I was experiencing the power of Satan. The strength of it was incomprehensible. It was pulling me into the tunnel, and I fought for my life. I clawed at the edges of the tunnel. The terror was horrendous and all-encompassing. This was no dream, this was absolutely real. I could feel myself slipping into the tunnel and there was nothing I could do to save myself. I knew that there would be no coming back. No "waking up" from this dream. I'd be gone into oblivion. I didn't know why, but this malevolent entity wanted me badly. I cried out in desperation, "*Oh, God, help me!*"

Instantly the powerful force hesitated and then released me. I could see a brilliant white light approaching, then boom—I was engulfed in this light. I was surrounded by unconditional love, in the form of this light. I could feel my consciousness start to change as I relaxed into this love and started to melt into it. My next conscious recollection is of me flying away from the light. I saw a bubble ahead and it exploded into me—or me into it—and I was shot back into the bedroom where I'd been lying down— shot back in with such intensity that I actually flew up in the bed.

I was surrounded by a sense of all-encompassing peace. No fear, just total peace.

I got up from the bed and touched the furniture to see if it was real. There was a sense that it wasn't as real as I once thought. All the objects in the room were surrounded with a hazy white glow. I wanted to hold onto that feeling of peace forever . . . it was like coming home. It was what everything is really all about. I felt so connected to the light, as if there was still a thread that linked us together. At the same time, I felt sadness for the evil thing that I had encountered, the thing that chose not to come home, chose instead to run from the light. There was a feeling that I was connected to the evil entity, that we all were, that it was a lost brother, a fallen angel and a part of us.

This revelation was slowly replaced with a troubling impression that I had been shown this vision for a reason, that there was something incredibly important that I had to do. Suddenly, I was overwhelmed with sadness—there was something that people just couldn't understand—*why couldn't they understand it?* It was so simple. I had the impression that the world was going to drive itself to a point where humanity would barely survive. I sensed that we would make it, but by the narrowest of margins and only after much tragedy. The sense of peace was still strong enough that I wasn't scared, but my impression was that the whole experience had been for a specific reason.

I will never know if the alien beings had anything to do with what I experienced, but I wouldn't be surprised. Spiritual experiences are a natural part of being human. They don't have to be numerous; one is sufficient to change your life.

INDEX

ABOUT THE AUTHOR

Jim Moroney, IHT, BSC, CRSP, CSP, is currently the executive director of the Alberta Municipal Health and Safety Association, an organization dedicated to helping municipalities develop and implement health and safety programs for workplaces. Jim has been a speaker at conferences and an instructor at the University of Alberta, the University of Calgary, and the North Alberta Institute of Technology.

On August 9, 1987, Jim's life changed forever when he had his first conscious contact experience at a small truck stop just outside Winnipeg, Canada. Since that time, he has spent twenty years interacting with the aliens, studying their methodology, and searching for glimpses of their purpose, all the while struggling to stay grounded in the face of this astonishing new reality. Based on his experiences and research, Jim has formed some carefully thought-out opinions as to why the aliens are here, what they are doing, and how we must prepare ourselves for the changes that are to come.

Jim is happily married with two adult children. The family is currently based in Calgary, Canada.

Hampton Roads Publishing Company

. . . for the evolving human spirit

Hampton Roads Publishing Company
publishes books on a variety of subjects,
including spirituality, health, and other
related topics.

For a copy of our latest trade catalog,
call 978-465-0504,
or visit our website www.hrpub.com